THE BURN PITS

THE BURN PITS

The Poisoning of
America's Soldiers

JOSEPH HICKMAN

Hot Books

Hot Books books may be purchased in bulk at special discounts for sales promotion, corporate gifts, fund-raising, or educational purposes. Special editions can also be created to specifications. For details, contact the Special Sales Department, Skyhorse Publishing, 307 West 36th Street, 11th Floor, New York, NY 10018 or info@skyhorsepublishing.com.

Hot Books® and Skyhorse Publishing® are registered trademarks of Skyhorse Publishing, Inc.®, a Delaware corporation.

Visit our website at www.skyhorsepublishing.com.

10 9 8 7 6 5 4 3 2 1

Library of Congress Cataloging-in-Publication Data is available on file.

Cover design by Brian Peterson

ISBN: 978-1-5107-0573-9
Ebook ISBN: 978-1-5107-0577-7

Printed in the United States of America

This book is dedicated to all the military service members and veterans who served in Afghanistan and Iraq.

Contents

Foreword

By Jesse Ventura

It's no secret what a disaster our wars in Iraq and Afghanistan have been. The Islamic State is a whole lot more of a problem than Saddam Hussein ever was, and the Taliban sure as hell hasn't gone away. Let's face it, George Bush and Dick Cheney were the worst administration in the United States' history. They ruined the economy, they got us into two wars, and they left things a complete mess that Barack Obama inherited.

But just when you thought the story couldn't get any worse, along comes *The Burn Pits*. This is a book that will not only make your blood boil, it'll coagulate. I mean, blood-curdling isn't a strong enough metaphor. It's not bad enough that, since the Iraq War began in 2003, almost 5,000 American troops have died and 32,000 more "officially" wounded (some estimates place that figure at more than 100,000). Or that more than 2,300 U.S. military deaths have occurred in Afghanistan. Or that an estimated 320,000 veterans have brain injuries, and the suicide rate among vets is escalating by the day.

It's not bad enough that the entire fiasco in Iraq was based on a lie—that Saddam was supposedly just itching to use an arsenal of WMD's unless we moved on him fast. You'll learn in this book that Iraq did once use chemical and biological weapons, against Iran and then the Kurds – but the Bush-Cheney people had their reasons for erasing that memory and claiming instead that the threat was new.

Why? Because the terrible truth is, those Iraqi leftovers that ended up in the dump were responsible for poisoning *our own soldiers*. And American contractors were the ones who spewed it into the air. The top military brass *knew* about this health disaster, and looked the other way. It didn't seem to be cost-effective to do anything else – so burn, baby, burn.

I don't want to give away the whole story, because it should unfold slowly and infuriatingly, as it did for me. The author, Former Staff Sergeant Joseph Hickman, was a loyal member of our armed forces for 20 years. In service to our country, he earned more than 20 commendations and awards. Well, he's recently done his patriotic duty by exposing the murders of three detainees in U.S. custody at Guantánamo, where Hickman served in 2006. Now with *The Burn Pits*, he's blown the whistle even louder.

You've heard about Agent Orange in Vietnam, which resulted in tens of thousands of people including our troops getting cancer. It's likely you also know about Gulf War Illness, which the Pentagon now admits afflicts close to 100,000 of our veterans. That's a cluster of medically unexplained chronic symptoms such as fatigue, dizziness, memory loss, and respiratory problems. Some call these "delayed casualties." But try using that polite phrase on the brave men and women who are still being refused benefits by the VA's powers-that-be for the debilitating illnesses that have plagued them ever since serving their country. Instead, call them "*denied* casualties."

I doubt most of you have heard of Balad or Bagram, or soldiers like Daniel Mayer and Matthew Bumpus. You will now, and the stories will sicken you. You also may not know that KBR – Kellogg, Brown, and Root, a former subsidiary of Dick Cheney's Halliburton company – was the number one corporate beneficiary of the Iraq War. A lot of those millions were generated by operation of the toxic "burn pits"—and Halliburton shareholder Cheney was among those who cashed in.

In 2015 Vice-President Joe Biden's beloved son, Beau, who'd served a tour of duty in Iraq, died of brain cancer. But you can bet the big media haven't dared speculate about, let alone *investigate*, the real cause, which as you'll see is likely connected to being stationed at two of the burn pits. One of them was Camp Victory, which is beyond ironic.

The Burn Pits pulls no punches. You'll read about the Veterans Administration claiming that the soldiers seeking legitimate benefits for their health problems were either lying or making it all up. You'll learn about the buck-passing and how the military can't be held legally accountable for what's happened to the men and women exposed to a toxic soup at 75 different bases. You'll discover a few heroes, too, like the courageous doctors who've dared to speak out about how the respiratory ailments and cancers are no coincidence.

I served my country for eight years as a Navy SEAL, and my parents before me in the Second World War. We all believed in freedom and democracy. It took a long time for me to consider that maybe we *are* no longer the land of the free and the home of the brave, that money and power have corrupted everything America once stood for.

Can we turn back the clock in order to move toward a better future? I don't know. What I do know is that exposing the truth in books like Joseph Hickman's *The Burn Pits* is a wake-up call to all of us that we'd better rise up and reclaim our birthright as Americans. And maybe there's a Smedley Butler out there among the veterans of our ill-conceived wars who is ready to help lead us out of the quagmire.

Author's Note

In 1961, during the early stages of the Vietnam War, United States and South Vietnamese forces were getting ambushed and attacked by an enemy they could not see. The thick jungle brush in Vietnam was the perfect environment for the North Vietnamese Army and Vietcong to conceal themselves from U.S. forces. To combat this camouflaged war, the United States created a new weapon called Agent Orange, an herbicide that Air Force planes sprayed above the treetops to kill the jungle brush below, creating fields of fire where the enemy could no longer hide. Agent Orange was effective, and the United States used it for ten years during that long war, killing almost 20 percent of the country's plant life and sickening thousands of Vietnamese—as well as many of our own troops.

As soldiers first started coming home from Vietnam, many were plagued with strange illnesses and cancers that couldn't at first be explained. By the end of the war there were tens of thousands sick. It didn't take these ill veterans long to realize they all had one common factor: they had all served in areas where Agent Orange was sprayed. At first the Department of Defense (DOD) and the Department of Veterans Affairs (VA) denied that Agent Orange was hazardous, and refused to provide the veterans with medical benefits. It took many years and hundreds of independent studies on the damaging effects of Agent Orange before the DOD finally acknowledged that the U.S. military had inadvertently poisoned tens of thousands of its own soldiers.

Now, as American GIs return from new battlegrounds in the "war on terror," we are faced with stark evidence that the U.S. military continues to recklessly endanger the health of our fighting men and women. During the wars in Afghanistan and Iraq, open-air burn pits were used in over two hundred military bases to dispose of the enormous amount of trash that was accumulated by the U.S. armed forces. The waste that was incinerated in these open pits included highly toxic materials, such as metal parts, plastics, medical waste, and even human body parts. Greatly adding to the hazard, some of these burn pits were built on ground that was contaminated by mustard gas and other poison weapons stockpiles that were blown up during the U.S. invasion of Iraq. The open-air bonfires—which violated not only EPA air quality standards, but the Pentagon's own regulations—were supposed to be used only as a temporary measure, until trash incinerators could be put in place. But the burn pits continued to operate throughout most of these wars, with a number still running as late as 2015.

Today, thousands of U.S. military veterans and contractors who served in these wars are experiencing strange illnesses ranging from debilitating respiratory problems to many forms of cancers and leukemia. Many of these service members and contractors believe their illnesses stem from their exposure to the toxic stew bubbling out of the burn pits. And a growing body of medical evidence supports their claims. But, just as with the Agent Orange scandal, the U.S. military has so far greeted these burn pit victims' claims with bureaucratic skepticism and outright hostility.

In many cases, when service members reported the illnesses they believed stemmed from the burn pits, they were told by Defense Department doctors that they were lying in an attempt to get benefits. The Department of Veterans Affairs health-care system—or the Veterans Health Administration—has been similarly unsympathetic, denying the medical claims filed by nearly all returning soldiers who report burn pit-related illness, and flatly stating that their health problems are not service connected. Many of these sick and dying veterans have been financially ruined because their illnesses are so severe that they cannot work and have no means of support. Denied disability benefits from the VA, their agonizing health problems often continue to go untreated.

I knew nothing about the burn pits when I served in the military, first as a marine and then as a soldier in the Army and the National Guard, during which I was deployed on several military operations throughout the world, including a stint with the 629th Military Intelligence Battalion in Guantánamo Bay. But after leaving the service in 2009, fellow veterans began telling me of the medical problems they had been suffering since serving in Iraq and Afghanistan. Moved by their stories, I used the skills I had developed in civilian life as a private investigator, and started looking into these medical cases. What I found after putting together the pieces of these war veterans' stories was more shocking than I could have ever imagined.

These were the young men and women who had risked their lives for their country, the warriors whose service America claims to honor, with stirring parades and gung-ho TV commercials and fighter jet flyovers at ball games. And yet after coming home with severe health problems, these brave men and women have been treated like waste, something to be disposed of.

This book is an attempt to tell these veterans' stories, to make them more than just a case number to be filed away and forgotten. If you find these stories disturbing, I have done my job.

Chapter 1

A Soldier's Story

From November 2003 to April 2009, in a lonely area of the Iraqi desert approximately twenty miles north of Baghdad, the United States operated a military base called Camp Taji. The camp was located in what is known as the Sunni Triangle, which in the early days of the Iraq War was one of the most battle-torn areas in the country.

In June 2004, Army Specialist Brian Thornhill was deployed to Camp Taji for a one-year tour of duty in support of Operation Iraqi Freedom. Brian was twenty-two years old when he left for Iraq. He was born and raised in the small town of Snyder, Texas. He came from a tight-knit Christian family. His parents were hardworking Americans; his father was a sheet metal worker at a local factory and his mother a part-time clerk at a local dollar store. He had two younger sisters, Emily and Amber, and a younger brother, Steven.

Brian was a good-looking young man; cheerful, friendly, and quick with jokes, but serious when he needed to be.

He had blond hair and blue eyes, stood six feet tall, and weighed in at a muscular one hundred and ninety pounds.

Like so many other young men and women his age, the events of 9/11 affected him deeply. Shortly after the attacks, Brian made the decision to serve his country and joined the U.S. Army. He had been working part-time as an assistant coach for his local high school football team, and he thought the Army would provide him with opportunities as well as a personal sense of pride he would feel for serving his country. He figured that if he could stretch his enlistment to last for four years, he could save enough money, supplemented by GI Bill benefits, to pay for a bachelor's degree. With the education he received courtesy of the Army, he hoped he could get a well-paying job and would be able to marry his high school sweetheart, Lisa.

Brian enlisted on October 12, 2003, and was assigned to Fort Benning, Georgia, for basic training and infantry training school. After twelve weeks of combat training, he was stationed at Fort Gordon in Augusta, Georgia, and was assigned to the 3rd Infantry Division. Shortly after arriving at Fort Gordon, his unit received orders to ship out for Iraq. Brian's infantry unit arrived at Camp Taji in the unbearable heat of the Iraqi summer and he soon learned that for the next year he would be working as a guard in one of the many tower posts that ringed the perimeter of the base. Camp Taji was often attacked by Iraqi insurgents and rebels with small arms fire and mortars. Brian's responsibility was to continuously monitor a sector of the outer perimeter of the base from his tower, visually scanning his area with binoculars and reporting anything that looked suspicious.

Nearly every minute of every day that Brian spent at Camp Taji was accounted for, and he had very little free time for himself. Every day he woke at 5:00 a.m. and got dressed for duty.

He carried a fully loaded M-4 assault rifle and he wore a camouflaged Army combat uniform, a Kevlar helmet, and a Kevlar-plated vest that was stuffed with a first aid kit and five ammunition pouches holding one hundred and fifty additional rounds of ammunition already loaded in magazines. The combined weight of all this gear added an additional sixty pounds to his head and chest. After strapping on his gear, he reported for duty by 6:00 a.m. sharp, taking his position in the guard tower, where he would continue standing for twelve monotonous hours in the unforgiving Iraqi heat.

It was stifling inside his guard post. The tower was made of wood and stood about fifty feet high. The perch at the top was surrounded by walls four feet high—just big enough to capture the desert heat inside the tower and obstruct air circulation. By seven in the morning on most days, the temperature outside was already a hundred degrees. The weight of Brian's gear only added to the misery he already felt from the unbearable heat, and he seemed to sweat from every pore in his body. The swath of desert terrain he stared at each day was flat and dry, broken up by patches of high brush, as well as the occasional wilting tree. Day after day, for an entire year, he watched over the same boring landscape.

Even though the base had been attacked several times by Iraqi insurgents, his particular sector had never come under fire. That fact only made it more difficult for Brian to remain vigilant in his job. He knew his duty was important, but the days were endless and miserable. He sometimes found his mind drifting. Alone in the tower, it was hard to stay focused; he would catch himself daydreaming about his hometown, his girlfriend, or his high school days when he played football and ran track.

Brian knew that, just as sure as the day would bring boredom and heat, it would also bring a suffocating cloud of black smoke and white ash that would invade his tower. He had a good aerial view of the camp interior from up in his tower. About a half a mile away, he could see the flames dancing from the open-air pit where the base disposed of its trash. The inferno would roar to life each morning around 9:30. Thick, dark plumes would begin drifting toward him and then white ashes would float down from above, blanketing the ground like a Wisconsin snowfall. Inevitably, the smoke and ash would come swirling into his tower. His eyes and throat would burn first; then the sharp, chemical smell would make his stomach turn. He would choke and cough and eventually begin dry heaving from the smoke, all the while trying to catch his breath. The white ash would cover him from helmet to boots, and would carpet the floor of the tower. About thirty minutes after that, his head would begin to ache, a dull pain that built quickly, as if a little man were inside it chiseling away at his skull. But there wasn't anything he could do about it. He had to remain at his post, squinting through his binoculars, doing his best to see through the haze created by the smoke and ash, ensuring that his sector remained secure.

The smoke and ash that invaded his tower followed him home each night when he was finally done with his shift. It filled the air when he walked to the chow hall or the PX or his living quarters. He always tried to get indoors as quickly as he could, to alleviate the burning in his eyes and throat, but more often than not the cruddy air would follow him inside, flowing through open doors and into air conditioning systems. Sometimes, soldiers covered up their air conditioners with towels at night, to block the smell and soot, and by the morning the towels would be black with the stuff.

One day Brian saw his commanding officer on his way to the chow hall, with the smoke and ash falling from the sky as usual. Brian had been having a lot of nasal congestion and seemed to be getting colds all the time, something he had rarely dealt with as an adult. He worked up his nerve to approach his CO, asking him about the constant fallout from the burn pits and if it was dangerous. His commander assured him that while the air pollution was annoying, it was not harmful. Brian accepted his CO's answer—what other choice did he have? It was not a good idea for a low-ranking enlisted soldier like Brian to question the wisdom of his commander.

The one-year tour felt like five years to Brian. War was not like the movies or television, at least not for him. Guts and glory were replaced with three hundred and sixty-five monotonous days in a place where his worst enemy was not a terrorist but the rancid smoke and ash that bedeviled his days and nights.

After finally completing his time in Iraq, Brian returned to Fort Gordon in Georgia on June 29, 2005. He was thankful to be back in the States in one piece. But his health was worrisome. Though he was uninjured and whole, he was still plagued with nasal congestion and cold symptoms. Soon after coming back, his military contract came up for renewal. The Army asked Brian to reenlist, but he respectfully declined. All he wanted to do was go back to his hometown and start a new life with Lisa.

On July 17, 2005, his enlistment was officially over. He boarded a Greyhound bus in Augusta and arrived back home in Snyder, Texas. Lisa and his family were waiting for him at the bus station. They celebrated his return by taking him out to dinner. The next day, he and Lisa flew to Disneyland for a one-week vacation. It was the best time he had in his life. They walked through the "happiest place on earth" hand-in-hand, unwilling to leave each other's side for a minute.

They talked endlessly about their future together and how they never wanted to be apart again.

When they returned home from their vacation, Brian applied for a job at the local grocery store and was hired. He also enrolled part-time at the local community college. Lisa was working at a local bank as a teller. They were madly in love and saw each other every chance they could. In June 2006, they were married and they rented a house right outside of town. Life could not have been better for Brian and Lisa at that point. Brian felt like he was living the American dream. He had so many plans for himself, his wife, and their future.

Though his life was great in many ways, his chronic health problems had started to become an annoyance. The nagging nasal congestion and other cold-like symptoms that began in Iraq would not go away and he began to notice other areas of his health change as well. He had been a very active person prior to his time in the Army. But after returning home, he noticed that whenever he went for a run—something that he routinely did in the past—he would experience shortness of breath and he was not nearly as fast as he was before he was deployed.

By September 2006, three months after Brian and Lisa were married, his symptoms were no longer simply a minor annoyance. The nasal congestion was constant now and he felt short of breath throughout the day, not just when he exercised. His breathing difficulty became so severe that it began to affect his work performance. He often had to pause and take short breaks to catch his breath while he was unloading trucks of produce or stocking shelves in the store. He decided it was time to see his family doctor and get himself checked out. The doctor told him he had a severe sinus infection and prescribed antibiotics to take care of it.

But after the two-week round of antibiotics, Brian's symptoms remained unchanged. In fact, they seemed to be getting worse. He could not even go outside and walk to the end of his driveway to get his mail without feeling short-winded. He also started noticing a slight, constant, uncontrollable shake in his hands.

Brian decided to go back to his family doctor. After examining him this time, Brian's physician said he was concerned and he wanted some tests done right away, scheduling him for a workup at a Dallas hospital, 260 miles away, for 9:00 a.m. the following day. After making the long drive with Lisa, Brian underwent a battery of tests that lasted through most of the day. The doctors told him they would have the test results back in about a week and they would forward them to his family doctor. Despite their exhaustion from the trip, Brian and Lisa didn't manage to sleep much that night or the rest of the week. They were too worried about what the tests would reveal.

When the test results finally came in, Brian's family doctor called him to his office. He told Brian he had a type of autoimmune disorder. The doctor explained to him that the antibodies his body produces, which normally fight off viruses and infections, were for some reason attacking the healthy cells and tissue in his body. Brian's doctor had consulted with several other physicians regarding the test results, but none of them could explain why this was happening. Nevertheless, the doctor decided to move forward with treatment by prescribing Brian several different types of medications in an effort to prevent his body from destroying itself. Brian was scared and could not believe what was happening to him. He felt helpless; he was dependent upon doctors, people he barely knew, to come up with a way to heal him.

By November 2006, about a month after being diagnosed with the autoimmune disorder, Brian was too sick to work and had to quit his job. He simply did not have the strength to perform even light physical duties any longer. He decided he was going to file a medical claim with the Veterans Health Administration, which runs the largest health-care network in the country, including 150 VA hospitals and 820 outpatient clinics, serving more than nine million of the nation's twenty-two million veterans. Brian made an appointment at the VA Hospital in Dallas. He explained to the doctors there that his symptoms started when he was in Iraq and he thought they were caused by the air pollution from the burn pits to which he was constantly exposed. The VA staff took down his claim, conducted its own tests, and informed him that it could take a year or longer to render a decision.

At this point, money was becoming an issue for Brian and Lisa. With Brian unable to work, their household budget was tight, so Lisa took on an extra job as a waitress at a local restaurant.

As the weeks went by, Brian's health began to spiral downward even further. In January 2007, Brian developed tumors on his chest and under his arm and they needed to be removed. He started having debilitating pains in his stomach and hips. With Lisa working two jobs, Brian found himself at home alone most of the time, unable to get up and walk into another room without pain or difficulty breathing. His deteriorating health began to take a toll on his emotional well-being. He was short-tempered and agitated. He slid into a deep depression and started to take his frustration and pain out on Lisa. He criticized her constantly for not cleaning the house, for not being sympathetic enough, or for not being around to take care of him. He was given antidepressants but they didn't work. His failing health took over his whole life.

In July 2007, just six months after the first tumors were discovered, he developed a tumor the size of a football on his left hip that needed to be surgically removed. That procedure left him unable to walk for months.

In January 2008, he finally received the letter from the VA that he had been expecting for over a year, the official response to his disability claim. As he tore open the letter and read it, Brian was stunned. His claim was denied: the VA had determined that his illness was not caused by his military service.

Brian was infuriated and his anger and frustration boiled over. He soon became impossible to live with and Lisa left him. She loved him but she could no longer withstand the verbal abuse and the burden of taking care of him and working two jobs. She moved into an apartment in town, avoiding his phone calls or any contact with him. It was hard for her; she remembered the man he used to be. It hurt her to see what he had become.

Penniless and heartbroken, Brian moved back in with his parents and stayed in the bedroom he had as a child. He was extremely depressed and spent most of his time in bed, weeping. In September 2008, Brian was hit with another devastating blow. He was diagnosed with brain cancer. His mother took him for radiation treatments and chemotherapy daily. He lost his hair and a lot of weight. He was violently sick from the treatment and so weak he didn't leave his bed anymore at all.

At night, through his bedroom door, Brian could hear the muffled sounds of his mother weeping in the living room and his father doing his best to console her. He felt guilty for how much sadness and stress he had caused for all those around him. When he finally fell asleep at night, he would often dream he was healthy again, that Lisa was with him, they were in their home, happy and in love. In his dreams he was active, working, and going to college. When he woke up, reality slapped him in the face. He was sick and weak and in pain. He was alone and helpless. Brian wanted to die and was angry with himself for not having the courage to take his own life. He wanted death to come soon and take him. The same way the smoke and ash would enshroud him in the tower at Camp Taji.

Brian died on January 29, 2014, in his bed at home. The official cause of death was brain cancer.

* At the request of "Brian Thornhill's" family, I have used a pseudonym instead of the late soldier's real name.

Chapter 2

A Call for Help

The American media is very good at bringing home the heroism and sacrifice of our soldiers as they fight on foreign battlefields. We often see heart-wrenching stories on the evening news about those who have been injured or killed in the line of duty, so far from home and their loved ones. While we sit safely in front of our televisions or computers, pictures of the soldiers flash across the screen, showing them in happier times and places—at the beach with their husbands or wives, or in their backyard, barbecuing with their children and families. I believe these stories are important and I applaud the media for reporting them. Those who make the ultimate sacrifice for their country should never be forgotten. I also believe these news stories may help give these soldiers' families some solace for their loved one's death or extreme injury.

But what we rarely hear about on the news are those soldiers who come home from war suffering from less obvious wounds.

In March of 2010, I was the primary source for a *Harper's* magazine article about the suspicious deaths of three prisoners held at the Guantánamo Bay prison compound. Shortly after the article was released, many major media outlets around the world picked up the story. I began receiving phone calls and emails from soldiers who were stationed at Guantánamo and at other U.S.-operated prison facilities in Iraq and Afghanistan. The soldiers were calling to give me their support for coming forward with the story and to share their experiences while serving on detainee operations. I quickly realized these soldiers just wanted to talk to someone who could relate to their own experiences.

One evening in June 2011, while I was relaxing in my home in Green Bay, Wisconsin, I received a phone call from a former soldier whom I had spoken with several times before. This soldier had been stationed at Camp Taji, Iraq, where he had worked in detainee operations. Throughout our conversation, I heard him coughing and wheezing on the other end of the line and assumed he had a bad cold. A little later, after he was gripped by a wrenching coughing fit that lasted for minutes, he said,

"Excuse me, I brought some of the burn pit back from Iraq with me."

"Burn pit, what do you mean?"

"The burn pits in Camp Taji. That's something that needs to be reported on, too."

He went on to tell me that at Camp Taji—the same base where Brian Thornhill was stationed—burn pits were used to incinerate all the trash accumulated on the base. He also told me that many soldiers in his unit complained of respiratory problems from the smoke created by the burn pits and that some of those soldiers continue to have chronic problems and are very sick. The conversation made me curious. I knew a lot of soldiers who deployed to Iraq and Afghanistan, but this was the first time I had heard of sickness related to burn pits. I asked if he would give me the names and phone numbers of other soldiers stationed in Camp Taji with him, who also believed they had been sickened by the burning waste.

I spent the next couple of days contacting the soldiers. I explained that I had been talking to a friend of theirs who was stationed at Camp Taji with them. I told them we had been discussing the burn pits and the health problems many soldiers were having after coming home because of them. I asked about their experience with the burn pits at Camp Taji: how long they were stationed there, how far away their living quarters and duty stations were from the pits, what kind of symptoms they were experiencing, and how their health was now. They all echoed the same symptoms and chronic problems, and gave me the names of even more soldiers with similar health issues.

Throughout that month of June, I spoke with soldiers who had been stationed at Camp Taji and at other bases in Iraq and Afghanistan that had burn pits. I explained to them what I was doing and asked the same questions over and over about the open-air pits. I became increasingly concerned with every phone call I made: the soldiers I spoke to were experiencing health problems ranging from serious upper respiratory problems to brain cancer, and none of them felt as though they were getting the proper health care they needed.

Soon I had a list of one hundred and forty-eight soldiers who had been stationed in Iraq and Afghanistan, all of whom were sick or, in severe cases, dying. All one hundred and forty-eight soldiers strongly believed their health issues were directly related to the smoke and ash they were exposed to from the U.S. military burn pits. Every one of these soldiers sought medical diagnosis and treatment for their symptoms at military hospitals and Veterans Administration facilities. All of the soldiers also filed claims for service-connected disability with the Veterans Administration. But the VA denied benefits in all one hundred and forty-eight claims, insisting that the soldiers' health problems were unrelated to their military service. Several of the soldiers I spoke with were even told by military doctors that they were faking their symptoms and lying about having them.

One of the worst stories of cold-hearted bureaucratic stonewalling was told to me by veteran Daniel Mayer, who served in the U.S. Air Force as an airplane mechanic for almost six years, including two tours in both Iraq and Afghanistan. Daniel now suffers from a rare respiratory illness called bronchiolitis obliterans, an inflammatory obstruction of the lungs' tiniest airways which can result from breathing toxic fumes. Daniel told me he first started having difficulty breathing after returning home from one of his deployments. He sought medical treatment at the Mike O'Callahan Federal Hospital, a military facility at Nellis Air Force Base in southern Nevada, where he was stationed. His doctors ordered a physical for him. After analyzing the results of the test, the doctors rudely told him they did not believe there was anything wrong with him. They told him they thought he was lying about his symptoms in an effort to receive disability benefits and then get out of the military. Thus began Daniel's agonizing journey through the military's medical labyrinth.

Shortly after his first doctor's visit, Daniel's symptoms became much worse. He started having coughing spells that caused him to spit up bloody phlegm. He told me he felt like the lining of his throat was tearing from the endless coughing.

Sometimes the coughing was so violent that breathing was nearly impossible.

As his condition worsened, he again sought help from the doctors at Nellis Air Force Base. But they again brushed aside his complaints, telling him that he was lying or that his complaints were a figment of his imagination. Since no military doctor would back up his health complaints with a medical diagnosis, Daniel was ordered to perform his full military duties as a mechanic on the flight line, duties he could no longer physically perform. Without support from his doctors, his command began to believe Daniel was faking his illness in an attempt to get out of work and they started giving him a hard time, assigning him tougher duties than he usually had to perform.

Finally, in desperation, Daniel consulted a civilian doctor, a pulmonologist. The civilian doctor immediately saw there was something very wrong with Daniel. The doctor wrote a letter to Daniel's command, strongly urging he be put on light duty and kept away from any industrial work environment until he could complete his diagnosis of Daniel's condition.

Daniel's command completely ignored the civilian doctor's letter and when the time came for the severely ill soldier to take the routine Air Force physical fitness test, he was forced to undergo it. At the time of the test, Daniel was not even able to climb a flight of stairs without coughing so hard he would get sick and throw up. Daniel attempted the test, but had to give up after completing only a few sit-ups. He was deemed by his command to be lazy and out of shape.

It was only after filing a complaint with the patient advocacy group at the military hospital regarding his mistreatment there that Daniel finally began to get help. Under pressure from the advocacy group, Daniel's military doctors at last performed a lung biopsy on him. A few weeks later, the results came back. Daniel was diagnosed with bronchiolitis obliterans, a rare and life-threatening disease. He was told that he would be medically discharged from the Air Force and that he would need to be plugged into an oxygen machine day and night for the rest of his life.

But even then Daniel's military ordeal did not end. While waiting for the medical discharge to be completed, Daniel's command finally put him on light duty. As he performed his new office duties, his symptoms grew worse. His lungs were failing and his heart reacted by trying to pump more oxygen into his body; his resting heart rate rose from the normal sixty beats per minute to 100 beats, then to 180. He was put on new medications to try to slow his heart rate. Then, as he struggled with these pulmonary problems, Daniel also developed tumors on his knees, making walking an extremely painful and difficult challenge.

Watching Daniel's health deteriorate, his immediate supervisor finally showed some compassion and told him it was unrealistic for him to come to work anymore. He told him to stay home and rest; the office would call if Daniel were needed. For a two-month period, Daniel was finally able to stay at home and tend to the grave medical problems that were quickly debilitating him while he waited for his medical discharge. But Daniel's bureaucratic nightmare was not over.

The active duty case manager working on Daniel's medical discharge found out he was not going to work every day and demanded a full inquiry as to why. Daniel started receiving phone calls and emails from the case officer telling him that he was abusing the system and that he was no longer contributing to the "team." The case manager asked the severely ill soldier, who by that point could barely walk and was attached to a breathing machine, "How is it fair that others have to make up for your absence?" Despite his impaired condition, Daniel was ordered by his case manager to undergo a physical assessment at the Health and Wellness Center on base to determine his work capabilities. Unbelievably, after Daniel's assessment, it was determined by his case manager that he could make a full return to duty. Daniel was in complete shock at the decision, and was afraid the military was literally working him to death.

Almost completely debilitated, and afraid he might die before receiving his medical discharge because of the work he was ordered to perform, Daniel reached out for help to Shelley Berkley, a Democrat who then represented Nevada's first congressional district. Rep. Berkley's office staff were stunned by what the service member told them, and they offered to do everything possible to help him. Just days after appealing to his congresswoman, Daniel received the medical board's decision. He was given homebound status, and was scheduled to be medically discharged three weeks later. Daniel's nightmare with the military was over, but he knows that the damage to his lungs—an affliction he is convinced resulted from the poisonous burn pits in Iraq and Afghanistan—will eventually lead to his death.

After hearing stories like Danny's, I knew I had to do something. Many of these soldiers were dying from their illnesses and I felt a keen sense of urgency to help them as soon as I could. I wasn't sure what to do though. I asked the soldiers how I could help, and they asked me to use my contacts with journalists to see if they would report their stories, in the hope that the press exposure would force the government to admit that the burn pits were hazardous to their health. The public outcry might compel the Veterans Administration to approve their disability compensation claims, so they could get the treatment and assistance they needed.

Frankly, I wasn't sure that I could be of any help. I didn't have proof that the burn pits were dangerous. All I had were the veterans' words against the military's. But there was only one way to find out the truth about the fiery pits. I began digging.

One evening, while sitting at my kitchen table with my laptop, I decided to do a quick Internet search on the topic. I was shocked by what I discovered online: hundreds of stories posted by other veterans who were sick and dying from ailments similar to those of the soldiers I spoke with. And they, too, blamed their afflictions on the burn pits.

Soon I came upon more than twenty class action lawsuits filed in 2008 and 2009 by veterans of the wars in Iraq and Afghanistan against KBR Inc. (formerly Kellogg, Brown & Root), the enormous engineering, construction, and military contractor that has become an indispensable corporate partner for U.S. combat missions around the world. It was KBR that operated the burn pits in Iraq and Afghanistan. The corporate colossus is a formidable legal opponent. A politically wired giant gorged on the profits of war, KBR is a former subsidiary of Halliburton, the company once run by former Vice President Dick Cheney. I printed out the legal documents from the federal lawsuits against KBR and began reading them.

It made for an appalling experience. The documents alleged that "every type of waste imaginable" was tossed into the KBR burn pits, including such toxic materials as tires, lithium batteries, asbestos insulation, pesticide containers, Styrofoam, oil lubricants, metals, paints, solvents, plastic water bottles, munitions boxes, medical waste, and even human corpses. In response to the shocking allegations in the lawsuits, KBR released a bland statement, stating that "at the sites where KBR provides burn pit services, the company does so...in accordance with the relevant provisions" of its contracts as well as "operational guidelines approved by the Army."

As I pored over the documents, I became increasingly determined to tell the stories of the burn pit victims, so their lives would not simply go up in smoke and be forgotten.

Chapter 3

A Disastrous Record

While I was trying to find out everything I could about the burn pits, I also started looking for relevant government documents; I wanted to find anything I could get my hands on concerning the construction and operation of the burn pits, particularly the health and safety regulations established by the Defense Department for waste disposal in the pits. I searched in public libraries for books about military base operations. I looked up documents about burn pits in military libraries and on the Internet. I also started filing Freedom of Information Act requests with the Pentagon. Within just a few months, I gathered quite a bit of information, and what I found was alarming.

I never really thought about or realized how much trash is created by war; I don't think many people do. Apart from the wreckage left by bombs and the other devastating machinery of war, there is the enormous volume of waste produced by soldiers on the ground, including everything from empty water bottles and meal containers to spent cartridges and worn-out boots. It is estimated that every soldier deployed to a combat zone accumulates on average about ten pounds of trash each day, resulting in hundreds of tons of solid waste a day being burned in the war zones of Afghanistan and Iraq.

The military practice of using open-air burn pits to incinerate trash is not new. Many forward operation bases during the Vietnam War disposed of their garbage this way. But during that war, American soldiers used canteens that they would refill at water stations. And they would eat their meals on reusable metal trays and plates with washable metal silverware. In today's wars canteens, metal trays, plates and utensils, have all been replaced with plastic water bottles, Styrofoam plates and plastic utensils—all of which are serious hazards when burned.

In the 1970s, as Americans became more environmentally aware, incinerating garbage in open-air pits was outlawed in the United States. Burn pits were still used on overseas military bases, but the Defense Department created guidelines for their use. In 1978, the DOD published a report titled "Federal Compliance with Pollution Control Standards," stating that open-air pits were to be used on military bases in foreign countries only as a temporary measure until an environmentally safer method to incinerate trash could be put in place. After the release of that report, U.S. military bases around the world did seek to comply with the new guidelines, putting high-temperature, mechanical incinerators in place.

But following 9/11, as the United States launched wars in Afghanistan and Iraq, the military was faced with massive waste disposal problems. The trash and rubble created by U.S. air strikes and the invading soldiers quickly became a serious issue for the military commanders on the ground. They voiced their concerns to the U.S. Military Central

Command (CENTCOM), the DOD's military command which oversees all U.S. military operations in the Middle East. The decision was made by CENTCOM that the best way to handle the problem was to construct open-air burn pits on U.S. military bases in the region. CENTCOM sent a request to the Pentagon to build the burn pits, and the Pentagon quickly approved their use—not just on a temporary basis, but for the entire course of the war.

Even more disturbing is the fact that the U.S. military— which seems to have a rule for just about everything—did not create any regulations for constructing or managing the burn pits when they were built in Afghanistan after the U.S. invasion in October 2001 and later in Iraq, when U.S. forces invaded in March 2003. By May 2003, there were over two hundred and fifty burn pits, many operating nearly twenty-four hours a day, seven days a week on U.S. military bases in Afghanistan and Iraq. CENTCOM put no health and safety regulations in place for these burn pits. No soil samples were taken before the pits were dug, and once the pits were operational, there were no emissions tests done to monitor the pollutants being released into the atmosphere.

Most of the burn pits were massive in size. Camp Taji in Iraq, for example, burned approximately fifty tons of trash per day in its burn pits. Balad Air Base in Iraq burned even more trash, roughly one hundred and forty-seven tons of trash per day.

Many of the soldiers living on military bases in Iraq and Afghanistan were housed as close as a few hundred yards away from the burn pits, and in some cases recreational halls and other base facilities were built nearly adjacent to the toxic pyres. Almost immediately after the burn pits became operational, soldiers started voicing concerns to their commanders. They thought the burn pits were an environmental and health hazard, but their concerns went ignored. When they returned home from their deployments, some GIs started complaining to their senators and congress members about the unregulated burn pits. Only after Russ Feingold, then senator from Wisconsin, and several other members of the Senate and House began voicing concerns did the DOD take action.

Finally, on September 9, 2009—nearly eight years after the United States had gone to war in Afghanistan—CENTCOM released guidelines pertaining to the construction and management of open-air burn pits. The regulations created in 2009 listed items that should not be burned in the pits, including plastic, paint, aerosol cans, batteries, medical waste, and unexploded ordnance. Unfortunately, because it took so long for the DOD to act on the issue, the U.S. military had already burned millions of tons of trash in the open-air pits from November 2001 to September 2009. During that time, most of the burn pits operated round-the-clock without any attempt to monitor and control the clouds of toxic emissions swirling into the air.

According to soldiers' testimonies and a 2010 investigative report published by the U.S. Government Accountability Office, from 2001 to 2009 the following materials were burned in open-air pits on military bases throughout Afghanistan and Iraq:

- Petroleum
- Oil
- Lubricant products
- Rubber
- Tar paper
- Asphalt shingles
- Tires
- Treated wood
- Pesticides and pesticide containers
- Asbestos
- Styrofoam
- Chemically treated uniforms
- Coated electrical wires
- Plastic

- Aerosol cans
- Gas cylinders
- Fuel cans
- Explosives
- Batteries
- Electrical equipment

- Medical waste
- Paint/paint thinners/ paint strippers
- Human body parts
- Animal carcasses

These materials, which were knowingly incinerated in the open-air burn pits and released into the atmosphere, contained over a thousand toxins and carcinogens combined.

Even after CENTCOM was forced to put the burn pit regulations in place, military commanders on the ground were slow to abide by the safety standards. The year after the guidelines were issued, the GAO report cited above found that U.S. military commanders in Afghanistan and Iraq still had not "established systems to sample or monitor burn pit emissions, as directed by CENTCOM's 2009 Regulation." Furthermore, because the military had done nothing to collect "information on burn pit emissions and individuals' exposure to burn pits, the potential health impacts of burn pit emissions on individuals are not well understood."

As a veteran, I was astounded and infuriated by what I was reading. At every U.S. military base in the United States where I had been stationed, there were always strict orders about protecting the environment, including rigorous pollution controls and up-to-date trash recycling systems. Burn pits of any size, including backyard fires, were expressly forbidden. Why were we so careless in Afghanistan and Iraq? Why had these huge, poisonous bonfires been allowed to burn year after year?

As I was reading through the burn pit documents, I vividly recalled the hellish pictures that were taken during the final days of the Persian Gulf War in 1991. As Iraqi troops fled Kuwait, practically annihilated by U.S. and coalition forces, they torched that country's oil fields. The ensuing fires were horrific; clouds of Stygian blackness obliterated the sky and rained thick drops of oil down on those below. Those oil field fires burned for almost seven months straight. The long-term effects on the environment and health of the population in the region from those toxic fires are still unknown. In May 2010, *Time* magazine named the Kuwaiti oil field fires as the "third worst environmental disaster in the history of the world."

I couldn't help wondering where the burn pits in Iraq and Afghanistan will eventually fall on that list of environmental disasters. How many lives of American soldiers will the burn pits claim? And how many lives of Afghan and Iraqi civilians, who lived downwind of the burn pits? There are thousands upon thousands of invisible casualties of a military establishment that could not be bothered to take care of its own soldiers, or those men, women, and children whom it was supposed to be protecting.

Chapter 4

Major Biden

Veterans of the wars in Afghanistan and Iraq have an odd way of describing the burn pits. They often speak about the smoky pits as if they were another elusive enemy they were facing in those countries. They also feel they were continually lied to by their command about the dangers of the burn pits. Many say that the only time they got relief from the siege of smoke and ash was when high-ranking generals or politicians would come visit their bases. While those VIP visits were in progress, the base commanders would temporarily stop the inferno in the pits.

After interviewing many current service members and veterans from all across the country, I realized the burn pits in Afghanistan and Iraq did not discriminate. A lot of people got sick from them: civilian and military personnel, enlisted and officers, black and white, male and female. It didn't matter who you were—everyone who breathed the poison air was vulnerable. In fact, evidence indicates that among the burn pit victims might have been Major Joseph R. "Beau" Biden, the eldest son of the vice president of the United States, Joe Biden.

In addition to his career in politics, Beau Biden served as a major in the Army National Guard Judge Advocate General (JAG) Corps. In October 2008, nearly two years after he was elected Delaware's attorney general, Biden's National Guard unit was activated for deployment to Iraq. Prior to his deployment, Major Biden was found by the Army to be healthy and fit, easily passing the Army Physical Fitness Test, which required him to do a minimum of thirty-four push-ups, thirty-eight sit-ups, and a two-mile run in eighteen minutes, eighteen seconds. He was also given an extensive physical exam just a few weeks before he deployed to Iraq at Fort Bliss, Texas, and he was found to be in good health.

In December 2008, Major Biden shipped out to Iraq with the rest of his unit. While in Iraq, he was stationed mostly at Camp Victory, which was located just outside of the new Baghdad International Airport. He also spent several weeks at Joint Base Balad, forty miles north of Baghdad. During his tour of duty, he was highly respected by both his peers and the enlisted soldiers serving with him. As the son of a prominent political figure, Beau Biden was a rarity in today's U.S. armed forces. Only about a fifth of Congress has any military experience, and only about 1 percent of all senators and House members have children in uniform. Major Biden's peers knew that he was, in the words of the old Creedence Clearwater song, a "Fortunate Son." He easily could have avoided going to war, but he didn't. Instead Biden chose to serve his country, right there in the unbearable heat of the Iraqi desert alongside soldiers who, in nearly all cases, had far fewer options than the vice president's son. As Major Biden walked through the base camps, younger soldiers would often go out of their way to salute him, shake his hand, and thank him for serving with them. During his Iraq tour, Major Biden performed his duties as a JAG officer at a high standard and set an example for his peers. For his exemplary performance, he was awarded the Bronze Star for meritorious service in a combat zone.

In September 2009, Major Biden returned home from his tour of duty to his home in Wilmington, Delaware, reuniting with his family and returning to his civilian job as attorney general for the state of Delaware. But Biden's life soon took a tragic turn. One day in May 2010, eight months after returning from Iraq, Beau woke up with a headache, numbness in his limbs, and paralysis on one side of his body. He was rushed to Christiana Hospital in Newark, Delaware, where doctors determined that the physically fit, forty-one-year-old Biden had suffered a mild stroke. After being transferred to Thomas Jefferson Memorial Hospital in Philadelphia, Pennsylvania, for a few more days of observation, Biden was released. But his health soon began deteriorating.

Biden started feeling increasingly fatigued and weak, and he sometimes experienced episodes of disorientation. Finally, in August 2013, Beau was diagnosed with brain cancer and was admitted to the University of Texas MD Anderson Cancer Center in Houston. There, he had a lesion removed from his brain and received radiation and chemotherapy treatments. Following these treatments, Biden's cancer went into remission and he and his family were filled with a new sense of hope. Less than two years later, however, the cancer returned and Beau was again hospitalized, this time at Walter Reed National Military Medical Center in Bethesda, Maryland. This time, his doctors concluded there was not much they could do to help him except keep him comfortable. Ten days later, on May 30, 2015, Beau Biden died at age forty-six.

A grief-stricken Vice President Biden released a brief family statement on his passing: "Quite simply, Beau Biden was the finest man any of us have ever known."

Unfortunately, there are many other tragic stories like Beau Biden's among the ranks of those who served with him. During Major Biden's months of deployment at Camp Victory and Joint Base Balad, both bases had multiple burn pits that operated round-the-clock, with no environmental restrictions. Many of Biden's fellow service members at these bases returned home with serious health problems. Army Warrant Officer Daniel Tijerina, who served at Camp Victory, later recalled the horrific burn pits there:

> I lived and worked under a mile away from where KBR and Halliburton operated open-air burn pits sites which produced toxic smoke, ash, and fumes generated through the disposal of waste in open-air burn pits. The toxic smoke and smell would routinely hover over the Camp Victory complex during the late-night and early-morning hours, because temperature inversions kept the plume on the surface or just above. I believe that I also ingested various amounts of toxins through food sources because of smoke plume dispersion through Camp Victory facilities. Camp Victory and [the] nearby cluster of military camps did not have clean-burning incinerators, or other [safe] methods for disposal of all waste at these open burn pits in place. KBR and Halliburton burned vast quantities of unsorted waste in enormous open-air burn pits with no safety controls. The open-air burn pits . . . created a vast amount of smoke and smell . . . [that] blew over and inside Camp Victory facilities, such as work stations, several dining facilities, medical

facilities, personal hygiene facilities, and living areas. Jet fuel was used to start the burn pit fires. Waste that was burned by KBR and Halliburton contractors included animal carcasses, asbestos insulation, biohaz-ard materials, cleaning supplies, dangerous chemicals, hydraulic fluids, items containing pesticides, incom-plete combustion by-products, human waste, a variety of chemicals, lacquers, lithium batteries, medical supplies (including those used during small-pox inoculations), medical and hazardous electronic waste, metals, human corpses, munitions boxes, paints and paint strippers, paper/cardboard, petroleum-oil-lubricating products, rubbers, office equipment such as copiers, printers, monitors, glues, and adhesives, plastic water bottles, polyvinyl chloride pipes, rubber, solvents, Styrofoam, tires, trucks, and wood.

As hard as it may be to imagine, the burn pits at Balad—the other base where Major Biden was stationed—were widely considered to be even worse than those at Camp Victory.

Just like Beau Biden, many service members stationed at those two bases during that time frame were in perfect health prior to being sent to Iraq. After their deployment, they became seriously ill. Just from my own research, I contacted one hundred and twelve service members and contractors who were stationed at Camp Victory and Joint Base Balad. Some were stationed at these bases at the same time that Major Biden was there. They all became very ill from what they believe was their exposure to the burn pits. Shockingly, of those one hundred and twelve service mem-bers, thirty-one suffer from different forms of cancers and brain tumors. Among those deployed at Camp Victory and Balad who later suffered problems similar to Beau Biden are:

* Specialist Emilye Rainwater from Sahuarita, Arizona, who served at the same time as Beau Biden at Balad in 2009. After coming home from Iraq, she was diagnosed with acute myeloid leukemia. She is fighting for her life and is on a waiting list for a stem cell transplant.

* Specialist David Green from Oklahoma, who was stationed at Balad in 2006. Shortly after coming home, Green started getting serious headaches and experiencing numbness in his limbs. Later he, too, was diagnosed with brain cancer and is still fighting for his life.

* Air Force Major Kevin Wilkins from Florida. He was in perfect health before he deployed to Iraq, where he was stationed at Balad in 2007. After coming home from Iraq, he developed brain cancer and died two years later.

* Lieutenant Colonel Michele Pearce from Virginia, who was stationed at Camp Victory in 2006. After coming home from her deployment, she developed two rare forms of cancers, and has undergone multiple surgeries and chemotherapy.

Sadly, the list goes on. One thing these brave service members have in common is that they were all stationed at Camp Victory, Joint Base Balad, or both. Now they are sick, dying, or already dead from illnesses that they all believe were caused by their prolonged exposure to the burn pits on those bases.

These service members' suspicions are supported by research conducted in 2014 by Dr. Anthony Szema, at Stony Brook University School of Medicine on Long Island, New York. Dr. Szema's research team conducted lung biopsies on several service members who were stationed at Camp Victory, and very high levels of titanium were found in all of the veterans' lungs. Dr. Szema strongly believes the titanium dust particles found in the soldiers came directly from the burn pits.

Titanium can easily spread to the brain through inhalation, and high concentrations of titanium can cause brain damage. Titanium has also been labeled by the National Institutes of Health as a possible carcinogen. Another medical survey conducted by Dr. Anthony Szema found that service members who were deployed to Afghanistan and Iraq have a much higher rate of cancer and leukemia than soldiers who never served in those countries. The rate of having a child with birth defects is also three times higher for service members who served in those countries than those who did not.

American soldiers are not the only burn pit victims. The burn pits were also a health disaster for the people of Iraq and Afghanistan who lived in the vicinity of these toxic infernos.

Chapter 5

"Iraq Is Poisoned"

While this book primarily focuses on the illnesses of service members who were exposed to the burn pits in Afghanistan and Iraq, the toxic fumes billowing night and day from these waste disposal sites also affected the health of the civilian populations in these war zones. As early as 2010, when the last of the coalition forces were leaving Iraq, the newly formed Iraqi government began voicing its concerns over reports coming in from health-care workers across the country. These reports indicated that the Iraqi population was suffering a sharp rise in cancer rates and birth defects.

According to Iraqi government statistics, before the first Gulf War in 1991, the rate of cancer cases in Iraq was forty out of every one hundred thousand people. By 1995, after the neighboring Kuwaiti oil fields were set on fire, the cancer rate ballooned to eight hundred per every one hundred thousand people. In 2005, two years after the Iraq war began, the numbers had grown to a staggering sixteen hundred per every one hundred thousand people, or twice the rate prior to the 2003 U.S. invasion.

Equally horrifying is the skyrocketing number of birth defects in Iraq. According to a 2012 study conducted by the Bulletin of Environmental Contamination and Toxicology, babies born during 2011 in Basra—Iraq's second largest city and the site of intense fighting during the invasion—were seventeen times more likely to suffer birth defects than those born in 2005. Rates of childhood leukemia and overall cancer rates also soared in Basra after the invasion.

Studies conducted in other war-devastated Iraqi cities such as Fallujah show similarly steep rates of birth defects and cancers. A 2010 study authored by Fallujah General Hospital pediatric specialist Dr. Samira Alani found the rate of heart defects in Fallujah to be thirteen times higher than those found in Europe. And the rate of local birth defects was a shocking thirty-three times higher than in Europe. "We have all kinds of defects now, ranging from congenital heart disease to severe physical abnormalities, both in numbers you cannot imagine," stated Dr. Alani. The birth defect rates in Fallujah have risen so sharply, according to an Al Jazeera report, that many city residents have decided not to have children for fear of the shocking number of miscarriages, infant deaths and deformed or otherwise sick newborns. Many of the birth defects being seen in Iraqi hospitals are so rare that there is no medical term for them.

Concerned about the birth defects plaguing her country, Dr. Alani met with physicians in Japan who are knowledgeable about the lingering health effects from the atomic bombs dropped by the United States on Hiroshima and Nagasaki during World War II. To her surprise, Dr. Alani learned that the birth defect rates in those two Japanese cities following the devastating nuclear attacks were between

1 and 2 percent, while her own case logs showed a far higher rate—almost 15 percent—for babies born in Fallujah.

As evidence mounted about the terrible impact of the U.S. invasion on the health of the Iraqi population, U.S. officials sought to downplay the medical disaster. In 2013, a heated controversy erupted in the international medical community over a report by the World Health Organization (WHO) that found that Iraq was not suffering an abnormally high rate of birth defects. "The study provides no clear evidence to suggest an unusually high rate of congenital birth defects in Iraq," the report concluded. The WHO study was immediately blasted by the authoritative British medical journal the *Lancet*, and by many renowned epidemiologists—some of whom charged that the United States had interfered with the study by preventing WHO researchers from surveying the most afflicted areas in Iraq.

Hans Von Sponeck, the former assistant secretary general of the United Nations and senior UN humanitarian official in Iraq, was among those who suggested that the U.S. had interfered with the study. "Everybody was expecting a proper, professional scientific paper, with properly scrutinized and checkable empirical data," Von Sponeck commented. "Although I would be guarded about jumping to conclusions, WHO cannot be surprised if people ask questions about whether the body is giving into bilateral political pressures. There is definitive evidence of an alarming rise in birth defects, leukemia, cancer, and other carcinogenic diseases in Iraq after the war. Looking at the stark difference between previous descriptions of the WHO study's findings and this new report, it seems that someone, somewhere, clumsily decided that they would not release these damning findings, but instead obscure them."

One of the most prominent critics of the WHO report was Dr. Mozhgan Savabieasfahani, a widely respected Iraqi environmental toxicologist who is now based in Ann Arbor, Michigan. "Iraq is poisoned," Dr. Savabieasfahani has flatly stated. The toxicologist, who won the prestigious Rachel Carson prize in 2015 for her environmental work, began her study of the war's impact in 2009 by collecting hair, nail, and teeth samples of Iraqi children who were born with defects, finding very high levels of mercury, lead, titanium and various toxic metals in the children.

Of course, modern wars are filled with many environmental hazards. Some medical experts, for instance, believe that ammunition containing depleted uranium—widely used by U.S. forces in Iraq—bears major responsibility for the Iraqi health crisis. But Dr. Savabieasfahani is among those who argue that the burn pits are the primary source of Iraq's health woes. Researchers, she has pointed out, found the same high levels of titanium and magnesium in the lung tissues of U.S. soldiers stationed in Iraq as they did in the children of Hawijah, a city taken over by American forces in 2003.

Among the most shocking examples of the havoc wreaked on the Iraqi population by the U.S. invasion, according to these medical researchers, can be found in the Hawaaza district, where the population suffers from extremely high rates of cancer and leukemia, and about one in four babies is born with disabilities. The villages in Hawaaza with the highest rates of cancers and birth defects are the ones that were immediately downwind of a U.S. Army forward operation base called FOB McHenry, where a large burn pit sent toxic clouds into the air from 2003 to 2010.

While it is difficult to address the health crisis in Iraq because so many of its medical personnel have fled the country, Afghanistan is even more unstable. Researchers there confront major obstacles simply collecting medical data.

With much of the country contested terrain, and terrorist attacks from the Taliban and other hostile groups a constant threat, collecting the data is dangerous work. Though virtually no current epidemiological studies have been conducted in Afghanistan, I was able to find a reference to one cancer report. In an Afghanistan government news release dated February 4, 2015, Public Health Minister Ferozuddin Feroz reported that cancer rates are rising in that country at a rate that its medical system cannot handle. Feroz estimated that there were roughly twenty thousand cancer patients being treated in Afghanistan at that time. Since the nation lacks the medical staff, facilities, and medicine to treat these patients, approximately sixteen thousand people are dying from cancer annually in Afghanistan. Public health officials point to pollution from years of unrelenting war as one of the major causes of the cancer epidemic there.

The outrage felt by many armed forces members who were poisoned while serving in Afghanistan and Iraq is certainly shared by many thousands of civilians in those war-ravaged countries. The U.S. forces that invaded these people's homelands were there to liberate them—that's what they were told. But these nations will be forced to grapple with the toxic legacies of these wars for decades to come. The victims of this growing environmental disaster—at home and abroad—are demanding answers. Who is responsible for these wars' hidden casualties? And who will care for those who continue to suffer the poisonous consequences of these conflicts?

Chapter 6

U.S. Army Inc.

Soon after I started looking into the burn pits, I came to realize it does not take a scientist to come to the conclusion that open-air burn pits are both an environmental hazard and a health hazard. I thought about all of the information I had gathered regarding the burn pits and was puzzled. I knew that burn pits were illegal in the United States. I also knew that according to the DOD's own regulations, burn pits were to be used overseas only as a temporary measure. My question then was, why did the Pentagon ignore its own rules and build so many burn pits for permanent use in both Afghanistan and Iraq? The answer lies in the old Latin adage "Cui bono?" or "Who benefits?"—the key question asked by investigators of crimes since the days of ancient Rome. Who profited from constructing and operating these toxic infernos?

Over the past three decades, the U.S. military has outsourced much of its operational functions to private contractors. In 1985, the U.S. Army created a program called the Logistics Civil Augmentation Program (LOGCAP), which was aimed at freeing up soldiers to perform combat duties by handing over to contractors such logistical support duties as laundry service, equipment transportation, and dining facility operations. This privatization of military duties fit the Reagan ethic of the time, which saw the private sector as a more efficient manager of the nation's business, even when it came to waging war. When President George W. Bush decided to invade Afghanistan and Iraq, his administration turned to Halliburton—the gigantic engineering and construction company that was run by Dick Cheney before he became Bush's vice president—and to KBR, then a subsidiary of Halliburton.

Halliburton, which employs over one hundred thousand people, is one of the largest corporations in the world. The company primarily focuses on work in oil field services, such as pipelines, offshore drilling, and refinery construction and operation. Halliburton is such a huge behemoth that it is headquartered in two locations: Houston, Texas, and the United Arab Emirates. Halliburton also has satellite offices in seventeen states and forty-one countries around the world and owns hundreds of subsidiary companies.

Halliburton and its former subsidiary, KBR, were the recipients of the very first civilian contract for the war in Afghanistan, a no-bid, $50 million dollar contract. This set the pattern for a flow of lucrative, insider deals throughout that war as well as Operation Iraqi Freedom. Among KBR's first assignments in Afghanistan were to build dozens of open-air burn pits for U.S. military bases there. After construction was completed, the company was then given the job of operating the burn pits and disposing of all trash accumulated by the U.S. armed forces in Afghanistan.

Later, in the run-up to the Iraq war in 2003, Halliburton was awarded a much bigger contract, totaling $7 billion—a contract on which, once again, only Cheney's former company was allowed to bid. Included in Halliburton's huge Iraq contract was the assignment, given to its subsidiary KBR, to construct and operate all burn pits on U.S. military bases in that country as well.

While the military was awarding Halliburton and KBR with these highly profitable jobs in Afghanistan and Iraq, Vice President Cheney—who served as chairman and CEO of Halliburton from 1995 to 2000, when he joined the Bush presidential ticket—continued to receive nearly $400,000 in deferred compensation from Halliburton. In addition, when he left Halliburton to join the GOP ticket, Cheney received a corporate severance package worth $36 million. The Bush-Cheney war years were particularly rewarding ones for Halliburton, as well as for Cheney personally. After a decade of war, Halliburton's KBR subsidiary alone (which was spun off from its parent company in 2007) reaped nearly $40 billion from its military contracts in Iraq, making it the number one corporate beneficiary of that war, while receiving billions more from its work in Afghanistan. These windfalls from war quadrupled the value of Halliburton's stock, which in turn further enriched Vice President Cheney, whose severance package included over $20 million in stock options.

This KBR bonanza has come at the expense of American taxpayers, who, according to government audits, have been forced to pay millions of dollars for bogus KBR billing, graft, and kickbacks. For instance, after the troop drawdown in Iraq began, federal auditors found that KBR continued to bill the government for unnecessary personnel—phantom charges that rose to at least $193 million and perhaps as much as $300 million. Even after these shocking revelations about

KBR corruption, Washington continued to rely on KBR as a leading war contractor. As Representative Christopher Shays (R-Conn.), who cochaired a congressional investigation into post-9/11 war profiteering, grimly explained: "We basically decided that KBR is too big to fail, so we are still going to fund them."

The specter of the vice president of the United States cashing in on wars that he had taken the lead in starting was too much for many government watchdog groups. One such group, Citizenswork.org, charged that Vice President Cheney met secretly with Halliburton officials to help close the lucrative government deals with the company, which, if true, was a particularly flagrant conflict of interest. Among the sharpest critics of Cheney's profiteering was Rand Paul, who, prior to his election as a U.S. senator, delivered a little-known speech at Western Kentucky University on April 7, 2009. During the speech, Paul strongly suggested that Cheney reversed his long-standing opposition to invading Iraq after 9/11 for personal financial gain: "Dick Cheney said in a speech in 1995 it would be a disaster to invade Iraq, it would be vastly expensive, it would be civil war, and we'd have no exit strategy," Rand told his college audience. "He goes on and on for five minutes saying it would be a bad idea, and that's why the first Bush didn't go into Baghdad. Dick Cheney then goes to work for Halliburton. Makes hundreds of millions of dollars as their CEO. Next thing you know, he's back in government, and it's a good idea to go into Iraq."

So who benefited from the construction and operation of the toxic waste infernos in Afghanistan and Iraq? Halliburton and KBR did—and, of course, the company's former chief, Dick Cheney.

The U.S. government made it clear, as early as the 1970s, that operating open-air burn pits to dispose of trash is a serious environmental and health hazard. Considering this, it seems that the Pentagon would be careful to hire a company with a solid environmental record to operate the pits. Instead, the military turned to Halliburton, a company with a long history of environmental abuses. Halliburton has been charged with a variety of environmental and public health violations over the years, including one recent class action lawsuit that accuses the company of fouling its own nest. Residents of Duncan, Oklahoma, the town where local hero Erle P. Halliburton founded the company in 1919, have accused the corporate giant of contaminating the local groundwater for years with ammonium perchlorate while cleaning fuel from spent missile casings. The company privately acknowledged as early as 1988 that its cleaning procedures had poisoned local drinking wells, but it did not inform local residents of the hazard until years later. The lawsuit blames the water contamination for a rash of illnesses in the area, including thyroid disease and colon and liver cancers.

Halliburton has also been accused of wreaking environmental devastation abroad, such as Nigeria, where, in the late 1990s, residents charged that an oil flow plant operated by KBR destroyed the local fishing industry and wildlife in the area. More recently, following the catastrophic BP oil well blowout in the Gulf of Mexico in 2010, government investigators determined that Halliburton shared blame for the worst offshore oil spill in U.S. history. According to a presidential panel, Halliburton officials knew that the cement mixture they planned to use to seal the bottom of the well was insufficient, but still went ahead with the job. The oil spill devastated the fish, plant, and wildlife in the area and crippled the economy in that region for years.

This pattern of negligence was also on display at KBR's burn pit operations in Afghanistan and Iraq, according to several former KBR employees. One of those whistleblowers was Leon Russell Keith, who sounded an alarm about the burn pits to Senator Byron Dorgan of North Dakota. Keith served as a remote duty paramedic with KBR from March 2006 until July 2007, treating contractor employees at Joint Base Balad in Iraq. He later went to work for KBR from April 2008 to June 2009 at Camp Harper in Basra. Prior to working for KBR, Keith worked as a paramedic in Houston, Texas, and northern Alabama for over twenty years. While he was stationed at Balad, he personally experienced the effects of the massive burn pit that spewed smoke and ash for twenty-four hours a day, seven days a week. According to Keith, an acrid, dark black cloud from the pit would accumulate and hang low over the base for weeks at a time. Every corner of the base was enveloped by smoke from the pit; everyone who served at the base was exposed to the foul air. It was impossible to escape, even inside the base's living units. Swirling ash from the pit would seep into the air conditioning systems and the living areas would be covered in a coating of dark soot.

Keith recalled that his room looked like it had a layer of dark-colored flour over everything, including his bed, his clothing and the floor. He and the people he worked with called it "Iraqi talcum powder." There was no way to keep the powder out of their living quarters. He could often taste the smoke in the air at the base, both inside and outside.

Keith said there was apparently nothing that KBR would hesitate to throw into the burn pit. As far as he could tell, there were no restrictions on what could be incinerated at the base. The color of the smoke would change depending on what was burned; sometimes the smoke was a yellowish color, but the worst was when the smoke was a dark greenish color. On these days, the KBR medical clinic where he worked could expect an increased number of patients, all complaining of burning throats and eyes as well as painful breathing. The thick smoke was especially difficult for those working at the military mail office, which was directly across the road from the fiery pit. He also noticed that the smoke would be particularly bothersome to new employees who had not yet experienced what some of the long-timers referred to as the "Iraqi Crud."

The acute symptoms of exposure to burn pit smoke included, but were not limited to, nausea, vomiting, lung and sinus irritations, congestion, diarrhea and associated dehydration, and even some cases of individuals coughing up blood. At Balad's KBR clinic, which treated the hundreds of company employees at the base, Keith and the other medical personnel provided lung decongestants and oral steroids. Some of the patients were so sick from the foul smoke that they had to be transported to the U.S. Air Force hospital in Balad or sent to Kuwait for advanced diagnostics and treatment. If their health did not improve, these individuals would be sent home. In his estimation, at least 30 to 40 percent of the total patient traffic at the Joint Base Balad medical clinic was generated by the poor air quality.

Among the vast amounts of garbage incinerated in the Balad pit was the medical waste generated by the KBR clinic, including used needles, gloves, and bandages, as well as bodily fluids and out-of-date pharmaceuticals. The medical waste was sometimes soaked with jet fuel before it was set afire in the open-air pit. There were staggering amounts of medications purchased by KBR for the Balad medical clinic, much of which would expire, so Keith and the rest of the staff were forced to throw away hundreds of still-sealed medication bottles. Among the many medications he was forced to dispose of were thousands of vials of Celebrex (an anti-inflammatory drug) and antibiotics such as penicillin and amoxicillin—pills which he believes were burned in the open pit. Keith worried that some people who lived on the base might have harmful reactions if they inhaled smoke from the burning medications.

While stationed at Balad, Keith himself began to experience troubling symptoms. One day, he started having difficulty moving the small finger on his left hand. Within a few weeks, he found that minor tasks such as typing were becoming more difficult with his left hand. He mentioned this odd development to a coworker who half-jokingly told him, "You'll probably be on the news one day because they found the lost chemical weapons under your living quarters."

During his second deployment with KBR, Keith worked at the medical clinic at Camp Harper in Basra, which was under British control until June 2009. It was a small base, and he was responsible for the health of fewer than one hundred KBR employees. During his deployment there, the base was under constant attack by insurgents, but even so he noticed a vast difference between Basra and Balad when it came to disposing of waste. At Basra there was a mechanical inciner-ator operated by an Iraqi subcontractor. The clinic at Basra treated a much lower rate of respiratory complaints. Most of Keith's duties involved giving vaccinations and adminis-tering general care. There were days when no patients at all came to the clinic.

Halfway through his second deployment, when he was getting ready to take vacation, Keith advised KBR officials that he was again experiencing difficulty with the function-ing of his left leg and arm, telling them that he would see a doctor during his vacation at home. Back in the United States, his physician immediately sent him for a neurological exam. After a series of tests that included brain scans, nerve conductivity surveys, and MRIs, his neurologist told Keith he had suffered neurological damage and was exhibiting the symptoms of Parkinson's Disease. The neurologist explained to him that his particular case was atypical for several reasons. At the time of his diagnosis, Keith was sixteen years younger than the usual age for the onset of non-traumatic Parkinson's. In addition, there was no history of Parkinson's in Keith's family. Finally, there was a large discrepancy between the functioning of his right and left sides, which suggested damage from toxins.

Keith's neurologist sent him to the hospital at the University of Alabama in Birmingham for further tests, where experts concurred with his doctor's diagnosis. They determined that due to the atypical nature of his neurological problems, Keith's debilitating illness was most likely caused by exposure to one or more environmental toxins while he was working in Iraq for KBR. He was approved for a medical leave of absence that lasted seventy days. But he soon realized that his condition would shadow him much longer than that, forcing him to take medication for the rest of his life. Unable to pay for his rising medical expenses, Keith made a claim for government compensation under the Defense Base Act, which provides support and treatment for employees injured at U.S. military bases overseas. He is concerned that his condition will progressively worsen over time; the pain from the muscular contractions associated with his disease has become excruciating.

By this point of my research, I knew that I needed to talk directly to KBR officials to get their side of the story.

On August 2, 2011, I called the company headquarters in Houston, Texas, explaining that I was looking into the burn pits and the adverse health effects that many people returning from the wars believed they were suffering as a result of the pits' noxious fumes. To my surprise, company spokeswoman Sarah Ui Mhuirgheasa was perfectly willing to answer my questions. But she was much less willing to accept responsibility for the health hazards associated with the burn pits, insisting that all such responsibility lay with the U.S. military itself. For example, I asked, "Why did KBR burn items in the pits that are known to generate toxic smoke, such as plastic bottles and medical wastes?" And the KBR official shot back, "The military recognized that disposal of such waste in burn pits was preferable to disposal in the ground." The KBR official used the exact phrase, "The military, not KBR" four separate times during our brief interview. The KBR official insisted that the company followed all regulations issued by the DOD on burn pit operations, although she did concede "the possibility that a prohibited item occasionally made its way into a burn pit cannot be excluded." But then it was back to shifting blame entirely to the military: it was the Army that picked the locations for the burn pits, not KBR, said Ui Mhuirgheasa. When I asked if KBR ever objected to the decisions made by the military regarding the burn pits, or if KBR felt that the managers in charge of the pits could have been more careful, once again she insisted it was all the military's responsibility.

By the time I hung up the phone, I was disgusted. KBR is a company that wraps itself in the American flag, claims to care for the welfare of those who serve our country, and profits hugely (and in some cases fraudulently) from the wars that our soldiers fight. And yet, the company's spokesperson repeatedly refused to accept any share of the blame for the terrible health toll that its waste disposal operations have taken on our service members.

Clearly, this was a shrewd legal maneuver on KBR's part. If the company bears no responsibility for the toxic infernos of Afghanistan and Iraq, then the military must shoulder all the blame. And, under federal law, the military cannot be held legally accountable. So nobody is to blame. The precedent for absolving the military from all legal liability for health issues was established in the 1950 Supreme Court case Feres vs. the United States, when the court ruled that military service members could not sue the federal government for personal injuries they incurred while performing their duties. The doctrine also bars military family members from suing the federal government for wrongful deaths if a service member is killed. With KBR placing the blame on the military—and the military denying all responsibility—a legal limbo was created, and no one can be held liable for the suffering of our soldiers.

Halliburton and KBR have not yet been let off the hook legally. In January 2015, the Supreme Court ruled that burn pit lawsuits filed by veterans against the companies could move forward in court. It will probably take years for these court cases to be resolved. But in the meantime, I was determined to take the case for these sick veterans to the court of public opinion. I continued to investigate the growing health crisis—a scandal that one former Veterans Affairs official, Kerry Baker, has called "this generation's Agent Orange."

Chapter 7

Warning Signs

One evening in late October 2011, I was speaking on the phone with another burn pit victim who had been stationed in Iraq, and he told me about a married couple in Texas he thought I should get in touch with, Leroy and Rosie Torres. Leroy was a captain in the U.S. Army Reserve and had been stationed at Joint Base Balad in Iraq. His wife, Rosie, had been employed for nineteen years with the Department of Veterans Affairs in Texas. Shortly after Leroy returned home from Iraq, he began suffering from illnesses he believed were caused by the burn pits. Leroy and his family realized they were not alone in their suffering and hardship, so they started a small advocacy group called Burn Pit 360, to promote awareness among military members, veterans, and employees of military contracting firms about the types of illness they might be suffering as a result of their exposure to the open-air burn pits in Afghanistan and Iraq. The Torres family also wants to establish an alliance of military families, veterans' organizations, and health-care providers to lobby for the development of a specialized health-care model that can provide lifetime care for the victims of toxic exposure returning from overseas.

When I first contacted Leroy and Rosie in December 2011, I found myself talking to a warm and loving couple. They were eager to hear about the research I was doing, and they agreed to share some of the information they had gathered through Leroy's connections in the military, and from Rosie's tireless research and advocacy work. Soon, I had a list of soldiers who believed their health had been damaged by the burn pits and a number of supporting documents.

Two of the documents I received were particularly explosive because they demonstrated that the Defense Department was trying to hide the danger of the burn pits from service members and government officials. One of the documents was a memo that the public was never supposed to see, but was leaked by Chelsea Manning, the Army whistleblower who is now serving a thirty-five-year sentence for violation of the World War I–era Espionage Act for releasing sensitive military and diplomatic documents. The leaked memo, which was posted on the WikiLeaks website, was written by Lt. Col. Darren Curtis, an Air Force bioenvironmental engineer. In the December 20, 2006, memo, titled "Burn Pit Health Hazards," the Air Force officer voiced his concerns to his commanding officer and to the U.S. Air Force Central Command Surgeon General, warning of possible serious health risks associated with the burn pits and the lack of engineering controls in place for them.

Lt. Col. Curtis—who is a licensed engineer and had seventeen years of experience conducting health risk assessments—brought a high level of professional expertise to the subject. His memo stated the burn pit at Balad had been identified as a health concern for several years after action reports were submitted by the soldiers stationed there. Curtis also cited an Occupational and Environmental Health Site Assessment study conducted between January and April 2006 by the U.S. Army Center for Health Promotion and Preventive Medicine. One member of that assessment team described Balad's burn pit as being "one of the worst environmental sites I have personally visited in my ten years working."

In his memo, Lt. Col. Curtis found it "amazing that the burn pit has been able to operate without restrictions over the past few years, and without any significant engineering controls being put in place." He expressed hope that "engineering controls such as incinerators would be used to mitigate these hazards." Curtis also stated that in his professional opinion, "There is an acute health hazard for individuals and the possibility of chronic health hazards associated with the smoke from the burn pits." Curtis's memo was reviewed by Lt. Col. James R. Elliott, the Air Force's chief of aeromedical services and a licensed physician, who concurred: "In my professional opinion, the known carcinogens and respiratory sensitizers released into the atmosphere by the [Balad] burn pit present both an acute and a chronic health hazard to our troops and the local population."

These internal Air Force documents got me thinking. First, health concerns about the burn pits were clearly being reported up the chain of command—in this instance, as high up as the Central Air Force Command Surgeon General. There must have been other reports detailing similar concerns. Second, this report was written in 2006, but the official regulations governing burn pits in Iraq were not issued until 2009, three years later. By this point, the war in Iraq had been going on for six long years. Why the long delay?

When it came to confronting the costly task of cleaning up the waste disposal process, military commanders simply dragged their feet, putting the immediate demands of the war ahead of the welfare of their troops and the civilians they were supposed to be protecting. This bureaucratic sluggishness and flat-out failure to heed medical warnings was not simply a problem in the upper ranks of the Air Force; it characterized the Army's high command as well. Just twelve days after Lt. Col. Curtis submitted his memo to his superior officers in the Air Force, the Army's Center for Health Promotion and Preventive Medicine conducted its own study on the open-air burn pit at Joint Base Balad. This study was authorized at the highest level, on the orders of General John Abizaid, then head of the U.S. Central Command (CENTCOM). It took nearly two years for the CENTCOM report to be released in May 2008. The report took an astonishingly sanguine attitude toward the smoke-belching burn pit at Balad, finding that "measured exposure levels from burn pit operations are not routinely above deployment military exposure guidelines (MEGs) for exposures up to one year" and that "adverse health risks [from the pit] are unlikely."

How could this high-level report come to such strikingly different conclusions about the Balad burn pit than studies undertaken by the military's own health experts? Unsatisfied by the CENTCOM report, members of the House and Senate began demanding further information.

On October 1, 2008, Russ Feingold, then a senator from Wisconsin, wrote a letter to the new U.S. Central Commander, General David Petraeus, requesting information "on the possible exposure of service members and local populations to hazardous waste in Iraq and Afghanistan.

"While I appreciate the nearly overwhelming set of challenges we face in Iraq and Afghanistan," Senator

Feingold continued, "there is no excuse for exposing service members and local civilians to preventable hazards."

A little over a month later, General Petraeus replied to Senator Feingold's letter, flatly stating there were "no dioxin-associated significant short- or long-term health risks or elevated cancer risks anticipated among the personnel deployed to Balad," and referring Senator Feingold, in a circular manner, to the May 2008 CENTCOM study.

By the end of 2009, many other members of Congress had also started receiving complaints from soldiers and veterans in their states, complaining of illnesses they tied to the burn pits in Afghanistan and Iraq. Like General Petraeus had done with Senator Feingold, the Pentagon brushed aside the ensuing queries from Congress about the burn pits, simply referring the legislators to the same 2008 study. But the Defense Department was not able to head off the mounting concerns on Capitol Hill, and Congress ordered the Department of Veterans Affairs to conduct its own burn pit study.

Instead, the VA simply appointed an outside organization, the Institute of Medicine (IOM), to conduct a "study of the study," examining the 2008 CENTCOM report, rather than sending a research team of its own to Balad. The IOM team interviewed a number of soldiers who filed official health complaints about the Balad burn pit, but according to the final IOM report released in October 2011, the Defense Department withheld critical information from IOM investigators: namely, what exactly was incinerated in the burn pits. "Information that would have assisted the committee in determining the composition of the smoke from the burn pit and therefore the potential health effects that might result from exposure to possible hazardous air pollutants, was not available," stated the IOM report. "Specifics on the volume and content of the waste burned at Balad, as well as air monitoring data collected during smoke episodes, were also not available." Instead, the DOD simply provided IOM investigators with "generic information on waste streams for burn pits at U.S. bases in Kosovo, Bosnia, and Bulgaria."

By refusing to disclose the types of waste, volumes of waste, and air monitoring data around the burn pit sites, the Pentagon effectively sabotaged the IOM investigation. Without this data, the VA could not determine whether the illnesses that soldiers were reporting were indeed connected to the toxic emissions from the burn pits. Confronted with military stonewalling, in the end, the IOM team simply threw in the towel, reporting that it "found inadequate or insufficient evidence of a relation between exposure to combustion products and cancer, respiratory diseases, circulatory diseases, neurological diseases, and adverse reproductive and developmental outcomes."

But as the brass continued to block information about the burn pits, military whistleblowers like Lt. Col. Curtis kept sounding the alarm on behalf of his fellow soldiers. In November 2009, Curtis, recently retired from the military, appeared before a Senate investigating committee chaired by Senator Byron Dorgan (D-N. Dakota). Curtis told the committee that after he drafted his memo on the health hazards of Balad's notorious burn pit in 2006 and sent it up the chain of command, he ran into stiff bureaucratic resistance:

> I felt like my hands were tied when trying to deal with the constant complaints from service members exposed to the smoke. Most of these complaints, which included headaches, nausea, irritation of the eyes and upper respiratory complaints, were probably associated with particulate matter [from the burn pits]. Air Force commanders also called and asked what I was doing

about the burn pits. A commander contacted me to let me know he had airmen who had vomited the night before because of the thick smoke. In addition to the possible long-term health problems from potential carcinogens and other toxins, the quality of life for those thousands and thousands of service members who had to breathe the thick smoke for months on end was poor. Given the lack of action in ending the use of the burn pits at Balad, the most I could do was to let the airmen know the exposure would be included in their medical records upon redeployment . . . During medical redeployment briefings with each Air Force service member, the smoke from the burn pits was the issue of most concern for our airmen. These service members would request that the burn pit exposure be placed in their medical records because they were concerned about the long-term impact to their health associated with their exposures. After my return, the one common experience I have noticed when talking to my fellow veterans who served in Iraq is the burn pits. Everyone who served seems to have been near a burn pit.

The Curtis memo was not the only leaked military document that spotlighted the potential health horrors of the burn pits. In May 2012, Spencer Ackerman, at the time a national security reporter for *Wired* magazine, broke a story about another noxious burn pit, this one at the sprawling Bagram Air Field in Afghanistan, twenty-five miles northeast of the capital, Kabul. As Ackerman noted, any visitor to the huge base could immediately detect its fiery pit—"if not by sight, then by smell. It's an acrid, smoldering barbecue of trash, from busted furniture to human waste, usually manned by Afghan employees who cover their noses and mouths with medical breathing masks. Plumes of aerosolized refuse emerge from what troops refer to as 'The Shit Pit,' mingle with Parwan Province's already dust-heavy air, and sweep over the base." But, as Ackerman reported, the Bagram burn pit was not just an offense to the senses, it was a major health hazard.

The magazine article was based on a leaked memo about the poor air quality at the Bagram base that had been written "for the record" on April 12, 2011, by U.S. Army Captain G. Michael Pratt, an environmental science engineering officer. In his memo, Captain Pratt stated that weekly air samples taken on the base indicated that the air quality at Bagram was "unhealthy." He went on to state that "long-term exposure" to the airborne particulate matter "at these levels may increase the risk of developing chronic health conditions such as reduced lung function or exacerbated chronic bronchitis, chronic pulmonary disease (COPD), asthma, atherosclerosis, or other cardiopulmonary diseases."

Pratt concluded his memo by stating that if soldiers who had served at Bagram developed any of these health problems, "they should seek medical advice from the Veterans Administration health care facilities in their local area." The problem with this helpful suggestion was that service members stationed at Bagram—which housed up to 40,000 people at a time—were never made aware of the memo and were never informed of the dangerous air quality on the base.

If soldiers were to be fully informed about their exposure to the burn pits of Afghanistan and Iraq, I knew it would have to come from those of us who have served our country and those loved ones and medical professionals who truly care about our welfare.

Chapter 8

Covering All Angles

By early winter 2013, I had collected the names and service details from over a thousand armed forces members and contractors who were stationed in Afghanistan and Iraq, were exposed to the burn pits, and were experiencing health problems they associated with their exposure. Most of the information I obtained about these people included the dates of their deployments, where they were stationed, and their symptoms. The service members complained of dozens of different symptoms, ranging from severe, chronic nasal congestion to brain cancer. With this information in hand, I began digging deeper, to find out if these symptoms were related to these men and women's tours of duty.

I began by seeking out Professor Mark Denbeaux, the director of the Seton Hall University Law School's Center for Policy and Research in New Jersey. The center, which was created in 2004, consists of a team of highly trained law professors, lawyers, and law students who sift through, review, and analyze mountains of documents concerning various government and corporate issues in meticulous detail. The Seton Hall Law School Center covers a broad range of public issues, ranging from human rights violations at Guantánamo Bay to the recent financial meltdown of our economy. The center's exhaustive research is aimed at uncovering the truths buried within the data they analyze, noting inconsistencies between what government and corporate officials tell the public and what the facts and data actually show. The center's findings have been widely covered in the media, and their reports have been introduced into the Congressional record by various Senate and House committees and have been cited by the European Parliament.

The center was busy working on several projects, but I thought Professor Denbeaux would still take on the burn pits issue. Denbeaux himself had never been in the military, but his father was an army chaplain in World War II, serving under legendary General George Patton. I think, because of that, Denbeaux holds a special place in his heart for soldiers. As I expected, the professor quickly agreed that the center should take on the burn pits project. Denbeaux and his team of legal experts and students soon began working on a statistical study of the burn pit victims, reviewing where they had been stationed and referencing their medical problems to determine whether there were any anomalous health patterns.

Denbeaux and his team focused on a list of five hundred veterans I randomly picked from my list. I had gathered all the necessary information about these vets, who were from all over the country, including their ailments and their deployment locations. All together, they had been stationed at seventy different military bases throughout Afghanistan and Iraq, at locations where open-air burn pits were used to incinerate waste. All of the veterans were in good health prior to their deployments. All of them were given extensive medical examinations before shipping overseas and all were deemed fit for duty, with no pre-existing conditions. All of them also stated they were never exposed to any toxic airborne substances either before or after their deployment. And all of the veterans picked for the study now suffer from a wide range of ailments that they believe were caused by their prolonged exposure to burn pits while on duty in Afghanistan and Iraq.

A few weeks after Professor Denbeaux and his team began to analyze the information, some distinct patterns began to emerge. Seventy-four percent of the veterans reported suffering from acute respiratory issues such as:

- Asthma
- Emphysema
- Chronic upper respiratory infections
- Sleep apnea
- Shortness of breath
- Chest tightness
- Chronic cough
- Chronic bronchitis
- Chronic laryngitis
- Chronic sinus infections
- Sinus problems/ congestion
- Sinusitis
- Reactive airway disease
- Decreased lung capacity

The remaining twenty-six percent suffer from more severe illnesses and diseases such as:

- Hardened bronchial tubes
- Throat cancer
- Lung cancer
- Brain cancer
- Acute myeloid leukemia

(A list of symptoms and diseases of the subjects is located in the back of the book.)

The five hundred service members in the study all sought medical help for their problems after returning home from their deployments. Another dismal pattern emerged: many of the subjects reported they were mistreated by Veterans Health Administration doctors at their local clinics. In some cases, the doctors even claimed the service members were faking their illnesses to try to get benefits. All of the subjects in the Seton Hall law center study filed claims for disability benefits with the VA. On average, they waited one year for the VA to respond to their claims. None of the claims were responded to in less than nine months, and some took well over a year. Unfortunately this type of delay on VA disability claims is not just limited to the burn pit victims; veterans have complained since the beginning of the Afghanistan and Iraq wars about such delays, as well as the difficulty they have making medical appointments and the overall treatment they receive at VA hospitals.

The scandalous treatment of veterans by the VA finally provoked a national outcry in April 2014, when CNN broke the story about forty veterans who died while waiting months for appointments at VA hospitals. In the ensuing uproar, Congress put VA practices under the spotlight and Veterans Affairs officials promised the problems would be remedied. And yet throughout this media tempest, the VA denied disability benefits for over 90 percent of the subjects in Seton Hall's burn pit study.

Professor Denbeaux and his team found that 97 percent of the service members with the most severe medical problems had served at six military bases, all of them in Iraq. These bases were located in Balad, Bucca, Mosul, Taji, Tallil, and Tikrit. The heavy concentration of severe cases at these six bases came as a surprise to me. Was there something unique about the burn pit operations at these locations?

To answer my question, I began looking into the history of those six specific bases. On the surface nothing really seemed to stand out as unusual, but as I dug deeper, a disturbing pattern began to emerge. Prior to the U.S. invasion of Iraq in 2003, four of the bases—Balad, Mosul, Taji, and Tallil—were former Iraqi military bases. Those bases were bombarded by coalition forces during the initial invasion. Afterward, American forces rebuilt the bases and established them as U.S. forward operating bases (FOBs). Tikrit had been a large presidential complex built for Saddam Hussein and was subsequently converted into a U.S. military base after the invasion. Camp Bucca was the only base that was not a former Iraqi base or government complex. Bucca, which was near the town of Umm Qasr, was constructed from the ground up by none other than KBR. This base served as a detention facility for Iraqi insurgents.

What made these six bases so hazardous to the health of those who served there? The alarming answers began to reveal themselves as I explored the story of an Army sergeant who had served in the Mosul area in northern Iraq, one of the most ravaged areas during the war.

Chapter 9

Project 922

U.S. Army Staff Sergeant Matthew Bumpus deployed to Iraq as part of the invasion force in November 2003. He was a squad leader with the Charlie Company, 2nd Battalion, 3rd Infantry Regiment out of Fort Lewis, Washington. Sergeant Bumpus and his fellow soldiers were on the front lines of the war, engaging in heavy combat near Mosul, where their FOB was located.

Matthew Bumpus was an experienced infantryman who had served on active duty for eight years, the kind of soldier who was entrusted with special missions. The week before Christmas in 2003, an Iraqi informant told Matthew's higher command that he knew of a site that produced weapons of mass destruction (WMD), and that the weapons were being sold on the black market. On December 23, 2003, Matthew and his squad got the assignment: that afternoon, he and his ten-man team loaded up three Humvees and drove through the desert toward the location named by the informant.

Upon arrival, they were to search the area for stockpiles of weapons and secure anything they found.

When Matthew's small convoy of Humvees rolled up to the suspected WMD site, it looked to him like some sort of military facility, ringed by huge concrete bunkers that were covered in sand. Matthew decided the search would begin with those bunkers, which looked like a logical place to hide or store weapons. Ordering his squad to take secure positions, he walked toward the first of several bunkers, opened the heavy metal door, and entered. It was very dark inside the bunker and his flashlight provided the only light. Once his eyes adjusted to the shadowy interior, he saw he was walking through some sort of ventilation system. As he continued walking, the ventilation system opened into a large chamber filled with fifty-gallon containers of chemicals, and what he estimated to be over a thousand mortar rounds and several barrels to fire them. Entering the room, Matthew was hit with a horrific smell, a sort of chemical odor that he couldn't find words to describe. He quickly decided to get out of the bunker, retreating the way he had come in. Returning to his vehicle, he contacted his higher command on the radio, alerting them to what he found. His command immediately dispatched a CBRN (Chemical, Biological, Radiological and Nuclear) specialist to Matthew's location.

When the CBRN specialist arrived on the scene, he entered the bunker through the same metal doors and almost immediately came back out. He had instantly recognized one of the chemicals in the large room. The CBRN expert donned his full protective chemical suit—including over-boots, gloves, and a protective mask—and went back inside the bunker. The specialist was in the bunker for about thirty minutes before he finally came back out. He told Matthew he had tested the chemicals in the bunker, using a paper test kit and some sort of handheld electronic device, and came up with two positive readings for a nerve agent. He also told Matthew that the mortar rounds were the type that could carry a CBRN payload. When Matthew reported this to his higher command, he was told to stay and secure the site overnight and more CBRN specialists would be dispatched to his location in the morning. Matthew and his squad set up camp for the night.

The following morning, several additional CBRN specialists arrived on the scene. They spent some time exploring the bunker, then informed Matthew and his men that they needed to be at least half a mile away from the entrance of the bunker, where they should provide security for the CBRN team. As ordered, the sergeant pulled his men back, and began setting up his observation post in a small abandoned building in that sector. As they established their post in the building, Matthew and his squad discovered foreign-produced CBRN protective masks and chemical suits. There were also bags of syringes and large glass bottles of white powder. Just as they finished setting up their post, a CBRN specialist radioed Matthew, informing him that the initial standoff distance of half a mile was incorrect; instead, his squad would be wise to move about two miles away from the bunker. As the sergeant began looking for a new location, his team was relieved by another squad, and he and his men returned to their base.

Matthew was deployed to Iraq from November 2003 to October 2004 and the only time he was ever exposed to any type of WMD was during this mission on December 23, 2003. Shortly after Matthew returned home from Iraq, he left the Army and moved his family back to Roseville, California, where he and his wife, Lisa, were born and raised. They had decided to settle down and raise their children there, near their extended families. By summer 2006, Matthew had a good job at the local cable company, he and Lisa were expecting their second child, and they had a comfortable home. Life was going well for the young couple. Then, on July 31, 2006, Matthew was unexpectedly rushed to the hospital by ambulance for appendicitis. While the medical staff was conducting tests on Matthew, the couple was stunned to discover he had acute myelogenous leukemia (AML), a cancer of the blood and bone marrow. He was told by his doctors at the local hospital that he had developed this rare and very aggressive form of leukemia because his chromosomes were damaged from radiation or chemical exposure.

Matthew immediately had to undergo intensive radiation and chemotherapy treatments, and for the next several months he was bedridden. He filed a medical claim with the Veterans Health Administration in early August 2006. Matthew was adamant that the only time he was ever exposed to chemicals or radiation was on his December 23, 2003, mission to the weapons cache, and he described this in detail on his claim.

In July 2007, nearly a year after he initially filed his claim, he received a letter from the VA stating, "Service connection disability for Acute Myelogenous Leukemia is denied." The letter went on to state, "The evidence of record fails to demonstrate you are unable to secure or follow a substantial gainful occupation as a result of this disability." Matthew quickly appealed the claim and asked the VA to reconsider their decision. Tragically though, Matthew died from AML on August 3, 2008, while his claim was still working its way through the VA bureaucracy. He was thirty-one years old. Ironically, a week after his death, Matthew's wife received a response to her late husband's appeal from the VA. The letter, addressed to Matthew, stated that the VA would re-open his case.

When I first heard Matthew's story, it did not appear to me to have anything to do with the burn pits, but after extensive research, I realized it had everything to do with them. Five of the six bases that produced the worst health cases in the Seton Hall study were located in or near Iraqi cities—Mosul, Balad, Taji, Tikrit, and Tallil—that were known as major chemical warfare storage sites during the reign of Iraqi dictator Saddam Hussein. It was the U.S. soldiers on these bases who were given the orders to secure these chemical weapons facilities and then dispose of the highly toxic agents.

According to CIA documents I obtained, the site that Staff Sergeant Bumpus and his squad were sent to inspect on December 23, 2003, was a former chemical weapons processing plant. The facility had been operated under a top-secret program created by Saddam Hussein, called Project 922—the code name for Iraq's chemical and biological weapons production program. Iraqi scientists working in the 922 program researched how to produce mustard gas and other poisonous warfare agents in high volumes, and Saddam's regime tried to hide the program by claiming that the chemical weapons production and storage buildings were pesticide plants. But the program's cover was blown during the Iran-Iraq War when Saddam's forces used chemical weapons against Iranian forces, killing tens of thousands of enemy soldiers.

Between 1978 and 1990, Project 922 produced thousands of tons of chemical weapons, mostly mustard gas and the nerve agents sarin and tabun. The program's main facility was a large industrial complex about thirty miles outside of Mosul called Al-Muthanna. However, according to both CIA and U.S. State Department documents, there were several other Project 922 satellite and mobile sites in addition to the Al-Muthanna complex. Those sites were located in Balad,

Taji, Tikrit, and Tallil, as well as Mosul—five of the six locations that figured heavily in the Seton Hall study of burn pit victims.

During the period that Project 922 was in operation, the Iraqi military base at Balad was home of the Chemical Corps Directorate of the Iraqi Ministry of Defense. This is where the Iraqi armed forces trained soldiers in biological, chemical, and radiological warfare. The base was also used to produce aerial bombs that held chemical agents. After the first Gulf War, UN weapons inspectors labeled the Balad base "sensitive," and decided to periodically inspect the base because they suspected the Iraqi army was still hiding chemical weapons there.

Camp Taji, too, was a known chemical weapons research facility in the 1980s. It was also the home of the commander of the Iraqi Intelligence Service, Ali Hassan Abd al-Majid al-Tikrit, known by his notorious nickname "Chemical Ali." It is believed that Chemical Ali and his team used that facility to produce the mustard and sarin gas that was used in March 1988 to kill up to five thousand ethnic Kurds in Iraq and sicken thousands more—still the largest chemical weapons attack against a civilian population in history.

Tikrit was not only the birth place of Saddam Hussein; the CIA and Pentagon suspected that it was also the home of a large chemical weapons storage facility, up to the time of the 2003 U.S. invasion of Iraq.

Tallil was one of the Iraqi Air Force's major air bases located in southeastern Iraq, and was a chemical weapons storage facility in the 1980s. During the 1980-88 Iran-Iraq War, Iraqi war planes from Tallil used chemical weapons against Iranian military targets.

Finally, from 1986 to 1989, the Mosul Air Base was also known by the CIA as a site for developing chemical and biological weapons, as well as for researching and developing long-range ballistic missiles.

Was it a coincidence that the majority of American soldiers who had come forward with severe health complaints were located on bases where chemical weapons facilities and stockpiles were once located? Were some of Saddam's highly dangerous chemical stockpiles unsafely disposed of in the burn pits at these bases? Were some of the burn pits dug out of ground that was contaminated by the WMD stockpiles?

I realized I had another deeply troubling, related mystery to investigate. After the 2003 invasion of Iraq, the Bush-Cheney administration was finally forced to tell the world that no WMDs were found in Saddam's secret storehouses—the threat of which had been the primary rationale for war. Was that not true? Was Iraq, in fact, littered with old caches of poisonous weaponry? And if so, why didn't Bush and his military commanders eagerly reveal this?

Chapter 10

No WMDs in Iraq?

"Saddam Hussein is producing weapons of mass destruction." Those were the words uttered by former Secretary of State Colin Powell during his hour-long presentation to the United Nations on February 5, 2003, a little over a month before the U.S.-led invasion of Iraq. Powell's report to the UN was supposedly based on human intelligence provided by people on the ground in Iraq. He also cited several different types of "technical intelligence" sources, such as wiretaps of conversations between Iraqi military officials—conversations the CIA claimed were about the WMDs that the Iraqi military was hiding from UN inspectors. Powell also relied on satellite photos of suspected WMD production sites that were provided by the CIA.

At the end of Powell's presentation, most Americans—and many people around the world—were convinced that Iraq had started producing WMDs again, in violation of UN sanctions. The only problem was this was not true. We now know that Saddam Hussein was not producing chemical and biological weapons in the weeks and months leading up to the 2003 invasion. As journalists later revealed, the CIA was aware that the information about WMDs it fed to Powell was deeply flawed and that the agency's sources were unreliable.

The CIA's main source on the ground for the charge that Iraq was still producing WMDs was a man named Ibn al-Shaykh al-Libi, a prisoner captured by U.S. forces in Afghanistan in November 2001. Al-Libi was thought at the time to be a high level Al-Qaeda facilitator running a training camp in Afghanistan. Soon after he was captured, he was transferred to Libya, where he was imprisoned and tortured by Libyan soldiers. What the CIA did not mention to Powell before his impassioned UN speech, was that Al-Libi had recanted all of his accusations about the Iraqis' ongoing production of WMDs. Al-Libi explained that he had lied about all of it under the duress of torture, telling his interrogators whatever they wanted to hear.

It was not until June 2015 that Colin Powell, by then retired from government service, received an apology for being set up to lie and mislead the UN and the world—a deception that led to endless, bloody tragedy in Iraq. Former CIA deputy director Michael Morell publicly and personally apologized for deceiving Powell, saying, "Here's a guy who had a stellar reputation . . . and quite frankly that reputation was tarnished when he went before the UN and laid out the case. That case turns out to be wrong. Almost every part of it turned out to be wrong."

While Powell was left in the dark about the true status of WMD production in Iraq, President George W. Bush, Vice President Dick Cheney, and the Secretary of Defense Donald Rumsfeld all received accurate national security briefings in October 2002, informing them that the claim that Iraq was still producing WMDs was unsupported. Still, just three months later, during his State of the Union Address on January 29, 2003, President George W. Bush told the nation: "Year after year, Saddam Hussein has gone to elaborate lengths, spent enormous sums, taken great risks to build and keep weapons of mass destruction." Meanwhile, Cheney and Rumsfeld relentlessly worked the media in support of the president's allegations, trying to pump up public support for an invasion of Iraq.

Persuaded by the unreliable information and outright lies disseminated by top U.S. leaders, Congress voted over-whelmingly to support Bush's invasion plan and America's allies soon fell in line. Among those Democratic senators who voted for Bush's war resolution were Hillary Clinton, Joe Biden, John Kerry, and Chuck Schumer. Among the senators voting against the Iraq War was Bernie Sanders, who objected to the invasion plan on moral, legal, strategic, and economic grounds—including the suffering that American soldiers and the Iraqi people were certain to endure. (As Sanders observed during the Senate's war debate, the U.S. government was not even taking proper care of its wounded and sick veterans from previous hostilities.)

If the Bush administration lied to the world when it claimed Saddam was still producing WMDs, it was correct to suggest that he was sitting on old stockpiles of chemical and nerve agents. But for reasons we will soon see, Bush officials were much less eager to publicize the existence of these aging WMDs.

Shortly after U.S. ground forces entered Iraq in March 2003, the Pentagon and CIA formed a joint task force called the Iraqi Survey Group to locate, inspect, and seize all WMD production facilities and stockpiles. The Iraqi Survey Group was a multinational force with approximately 1,700 members. The group was first led by David Kay, a former UN chief weapons inspector, who had worked in Iraq in 1992 and 1993. Ten months later, in January 2004, Kay was replaced by Charles Duelfer, the CIA's chief advisor on Iraqi WMDs.

To the Bush administration's great disappointment and humiliation, the Iraqi Survey Group's teams could find no evidence that Saddam was continuing to produce WMDs in the months leading up to the U.S. invasion. But Duelfer's investigators did find ample supplies of old WMDs at various sites throughout Iraq. Many of those stockpiles were stored in bunkers and were sealed off in the 1990s by United Nations inspection teams. Many other old WMD stockpiles, undetected by UN inspectors, were discovered by U.S. forces after the invasion.

As the *New York Times*' C. J. Chivers reported in October 2014: "From 2004 to 2011 American forces and American-trained Iraqi troops repeatedly encountered, and on at least six occasions were wounded by, chemical weapons remaining from earlier years in Saddam Hussein's rule. In all, American troops secretly reported finding roughly 5,000 chemical warheads, shells, or aviation bombs, according to interviews with dozens of participants, Iraqi and American officials, and heavily redacted intelligence documents obtained under the Freedom of Information Act." Chivers also reported that he found at least seventeen American service members and seven Iraqi police officers who were exposed to nerve or mustard agents. He was told by U.S. government officials that the number of exposed troops was higher, but the exact number was classified.

If U.S. soldiers were discovering so many chemical weapons, why didn't the Bush administration rush to publicize this fact, to defend its decision to invade Iraq? As the country descended into chaos and bloodshed, Bush and his war council came under increasingly withering criticism for "cooking" the intelligence that led us to war. The president and his top warriors might have been completely wrong about Saddam's continued production of WMDs, but coalition forces were certainly discovering enough old stockpiles; banging the drum about these aging stacks of weapons might have given Bush at least some justification for his disastrous military decision. After all, the political damage to the Bush legacy continues to the very present, with Ron Fournier, the respected former Washington bureau chief of the Associated Press, flatly stating in February 2015 that George W. Bush "lied us into war in Iraq." So why did the Bush administration remain largely silent about the discoveries of old WMD stockpiles?

The answer to that question might have proved even more embarrassing to the Bush dynasty. Because the shocking fact is that it was the United States and its allies that provided Iraq with the bulk of its weapons of mass destruction—the WMDs that American troops were now tracking down and which, indeed, were sickening some soldiers. As the *New York Times* subsequently reported, during the Iraq-Iran War, when Saddam unleashed the horrors of chemical warfare, "In five of six incidents in which troops were wounded by chemical agents, the munitions appeared to have been designed in the United States, manufactured in Europe, and filled in chemical agent production lines built in Iraq by Western companies." Thus, Saddam began building his WMD stockpiles back in the 1980s courtesy of the U.S. government—which was then led by President Ronald Reagan, and, of course, by Vice President George Bush, father of the man who took the country to war over those very same WMDs.

This is not the kind of eye-opening fact about the war in Iraq that the Bush administration was eager to highlight.

And the ongoing WMD story has only made the Bush dynasty look worse as time goes by. As the *New York Times* reported in early 2015, one of the key centers of Iraqi chemical weapons production in the 1980s has now fallen into the hands of Islamic State, "the world's most radical and violent jihadist group."

The United States' shameful involvement in Iraq's WMD story dates back to when the Reagan-Bush administration was eager to support Saddam's regime against Iran. Washington was eager to take revenge on Tehran's revolutionary government after it humiliated the United States by allowing militants to overrun the American embassy in Iran and take embassy personnel captive. The Reagan-Bush administration sided with Iraq, even though Saddam's regime started the war by invading Iran in September 1980 and would later be characterized as the aggressor by the UN Security Council. Reagan officials went as far as to remove Iraq from the State Department list of State Sponsors of Terrorism, in order to facilitate the flow of military aid to Saddam.

When Iran introduced a draft UN resolution condemning Iraq's use of chemical weapons, citing the Geneva Protocol of 1925, the Reagan administration told its UN representative, Jeane Kirkpatrick, and U.S. allies to support a "no decision" motion on Saddam's shocking war crimes. According to an affidavit by former National Security Council member Howard Teicher, during the war, the U.S strongly backed the Iraqi regime by covertly "providing U.S. military intelligence and advice to the Iraqis, and by closely monitoring third country arms sales to Iraq to make sure that Iraq had the military weaponry required. The United States also provided strategic operational advice to the Iraqis to better use their assets in combat . . . The CIA, including both CIA Director [William] Casey and Deputy Director [Robert] Gates, knew of, approved of, and assisted in the sale of non-U.S. origin military weapons, ammunition, and vehicles to Iraq."

In 1994, Senator Donald Riegle (D-Michigan) led an investigation into the impact of chemical and biological weapons that the Reagan government had provided Saddam on the health of U.S. soldiers during the Gulf War. The exports of this dangerous "dual-use technology" to the Baghdad regime made for "a devastating record," declared Senator Riegle. But, he stated, Pentagon officials seemed serenely unbothered:

> Frankly, the Defense Department does not have too much interest in [a retired Army colonel who is sick and unemployed]. They are looking ahead to other things. They are not looking back at the large number of sick veterans who are out there. But it does not take a Ph.D., knowing Saddam Hussein's record, knowing he had the production facilities, knowing that we went in and bombed some of those production facilities, and knowing that the things that we sent him helped him produce biological weapons, to understand that such exposures may—I underline the word may—be causing the problems of a lot of our sick veterans that otherwise are defying explanation.

Saddam would, of course, also infamously use chemical weapons on his own citizens, the Kurds—a crime against humanity that George W. Bush would later invoke as partial justification for his invasion, though it was the administration of his own father, then Vice President George H. W. Bush, who supplied these horrific weapons to Saddam.

In other words, there were many inconvenient facts about the Reagan-Bush administration, the Saddam regime, and

the use of WMDs in the region that the Bush-Cheney administration was eager to sweep under the rug. This became
even more urgent as post-Saddam Iraq spun out of control
and the United States was forced to rely on the neighboring
Iranian government to help restore order in Iraq. Publi-
cizing the fact that President George W. Bush's father had
helped supply Saddam with the chemical weapons used to
kill thousands of Iranians would certainly not have helped
diplomatic relations between Tehran and Washington.

There was one final, perhaps even more compelling,
reason that the Bush-Cheney administration sought to
downplay the WMD story after the invasion. In the chaos
that ensued after Operation Iraqi Freedom, U.S. forces failed
to secure Saddam's chemical weapons stockpiles, allowing
militants to loot them and sell the munitions on the black
market. As the bloody U.S. occupation of Iraq dragged on,
insurgent forces repeatedly used captured chemical weapons
in their roadside bomb attacks against American soldiers.
Hence, as the *New York Times* reported in October 2014,
"troops and officers were instructed to be silent or give
deceptive accounts of what they had found" when they came
across chemical weapons. As far as the Bush administration
was concerned, these aging WMD stockpiles did not exist.

And the ongoing WMD story has only made the Bush
dynasty look worse as time goes by. As the *New York Times*
reported in early 2015, one of the key centers of Iraqi chemical
weapons production in the 1980s has now fallen into the
hands of the Islamic State, "the world's most radical and
violent jihadist group." A September 2015 article in the *Times*
revealed that traces of sulfur mustard were found on frag-
ments of weapons used by the Islamic State in Iraq and Syria,
although the connection between these weapons and
Saddam's old WMD inventories has not been confirmed.

So the Bush-Cheney administration officials had ample reason to cover up the WMD story in Iraq, and they did. But I realized the truth was still out there. I knew I had to get in touch with members of the Iraqi Survey Group, the experts who had scoured Iraq for WMDs, and ask them what they had found. When I finally tracked down some members of the team, it was hard to get them to comment on the record. Finally, one member of the group, Dave Gaubatz, agreed to speak.

Gaubatz is now retired from the military after serving twelve years in the U.S. Air Force's Office of Special Investigations as a counterterrorism specialist. He is fluent in Arabic, and after retiring from the Air Force, he became a civilian counterintelligence agent for the Pentagon's Defense Intelligence Agency. In the wake of the invasion, Gaubatz was the first U.S. agent to arrive in Iraq to look for WMDs. After locating the chemical and biological stockpiles, Gaubatz was to inform his supervisors at the Iraqi Survey Group, who would then dispatch inspectors to the site.

Gaubatz told me, based on his findings, there is no doubt that Saddam kept stockpiles of old WMDs, including one he personally located near Camp Bucca. But when he sent his findings to the Iraqi Survey Group, said Gaubatz, it seemed to him as though his reports either disappeared or were completely ignored. Whenever he followed up to see when the inspection teams would arrive at the locations he reported, he was repeatedly told by Iraqi Survey Group officials that they would get back to him. They never did. In fact, Gaubatz went on to say, the Iraqi Survey Group failed to inspect over 90 percent of the suspected WMD sites located and reported by him and other agents.

I asked Gaubatz how the Iraq Survey Group explained its unresponsive behavior. He said that the task force's leader,

Charles Duelfer, claimed that it was too dangerous to inspect suspicious sites because they were usually located near combat zones. As he recalled Duelfer's explanation, Gaubatz broke out laughing. "Now Staff Sergeant Hickman, have you ever heard of a war zone that was *not* dangerous? He should have thought of that before accepting the position."

The real reason the Iraqi Survey Group didn't want to send inspectors to the WMD sites, Gaubatz told me, was because in many cases they knew they were already too late, and the group would have been embarrassed to admit it. Many of the WMDs from those sites had already been taken by Iraqi militants and sold on the black market or moved to Syria. Gaubatz stated, "I believe many of the WMDs ended up in the hands of terrorists and terrorist states. The very thing the Iraqi Survey Group was supposed to stop from happening."

I don't know if Dave Gaubatz's theory is true. But—with the addition of what Gaubatz went on to tell me about Camp Bucca—I did know for certain that all six bases where high rates of burn pit–related illness had been reported were sites that had been pinpointed by WMD inspectors as former Iraqi chemical weapons facilities. These six areas—Bucca, Balad, Mosul, Taji, Tikrit, and Talil—had come up time and again when I spoke with ailing soldiers. They were all chemical weapons sites. And all of these installations were heavily bombarded during the first months of the war and then later rebuilt into bases where tens of thousands of American soldiers worked and lived. U.S. military personnel were stationed at sites that were contaminated by old WMDs; and likely, this danger increased when the burn pits were excavated from the contaminated earth, and the poison was further dispersed when the pits were ignited.

While our troops faced an enemy that often seemed invisible in Afghanistan and Iraq, the environmental dangers that surrounded them, on the ground where they walked and in the air they breathed, was equally deadly.

Chapter 11

"We Knew the Ground Was Hot"

There was a neighborhood near where I grew up, just south of downtown Baltimore, called Wagner's Point. It was over a hundred years old and named after Martin Wagner, an entrepreneur who established his food-packing business there with a small working community around it. When I was growing up, the community was comprised of about three hundred residents, who occupied ninety-three row houses tucked into a six-block area. It was a tightly knit, working class neighborhood, with many residents who could trace their Wagner's Point heritage through generations in time. As the years went by, Wagner's Point became an industrial site, with oil refineries, chemical plants, scrap metal dump sites, a sewage treatment plant, and other developments that provided jobs, but made the neighborhood less and less attractive as a place to live and raise children. On a regular basis, the district was smothered by foul odors and smoke, by-products of the industrial progress that was the neighborhood's blessing and curse.

By the 1960s and 1970s, public health officials noticed an alarming trend among Wagner's Point residents—they were suffering from serious illnesses, such as cancer, with greater frequency than the general population. Community members became activists and fought vigorously to get the government to condemn their homes and relocate them to an area where they and their families would be safe from toxic emissions and waste. Though residents had deep roots in the community and many of them didn't want to move, they knew their health and their children's health depended on it. Knowing that their homes were virtually worthless, since the neighborhood had become notorious for its toxic landscape and foul odors, those who couldn't afford to simply abandon their dwellings continued to press the government for relocation assistance. Residents put up posters in their windows pleading for help. By the late 1990s, most of the industrial facilities and local retail shops had vacated the area, leaving behind only toxic marshes and polluted, fenced-off beaches where it was too dangerous to go swimming.

When an explosion and fire erupted at a plant near Wagner's Point in October 1998, the area's remaining population found itself in an alarming position. Unable to evacuate the area because the only road out of the neighborhood went directly past the burning plant, the residents were forced to remain in Wagner's Point while the fire raged on, spewing toxic smoke and ash over their neighborhood. That incident, caught live on local TV, along with several other publicized chemical accidents, finally compelled state officials to agree to a buyout. By December 2000, Wagner's Point was empty. Soon after, all the residential buildings were leveled to make way for a sewage plant expansion.

I thought about the plight of Wagner's Point and its residents, so close to the neighborhood where I grew up, as I pursued my research on the burn pits. Government and corporate officials had shown the same callous disregard for the working-class people of Wagner's Point that they did for the soldiers on the front lines in Afghanistan and Iraq.

I now knew that the U.S. military and leading war contractors like KBR built housing for our soldiers in Iraq on top of areas where dangerous chemical war agents had been manufactured and stored. We bombed these areas heavily at the beginning of the Iraq War, and this almost certainly resulted in the widespread contamination of the surrounding terrain. It was already known that a variety of materials containing hazardous chemicals were incinerated in the burn pits. But what about the ground itself, where these fires burned night and day throughout the week—were these pits scooped out of earth that was already contaminated? Did this ground contain chemical waste from Saddam's deadly stockpiles of mustard gas and nerve agents? If so, the soldiers on those bases—and the civilian populations downwind from them— would have been exposed to particularly lethal plumes as they wafted into the sky from the fiery pits.

I took these questions to Professor Ralph Allen, the chairman of the chemistry department at the University of Virginia. In addition to his teaching duties, Allen serves as the associate vice president for research at the university and directs its Office of Environmental Health and Safety. Professor Allen has also written over one hundred papers, many concerning environmental pollution. When I shared with him the information I had gathered so far, the professor told me: "It is a real concern about what [the military] was burning, but what is even more concerning is that it is possible that a heavy bombardment of a chemical weapons facility could have contaminated the ground, and those contaminants could have become airborne while the burn pits were operational."

Professor Allen went on to say that soil samples should have been taken at the burn pit sites before construction of the pits began, and air quality tests should have been conducted while they were operational.

Allen's concerns are, in fact, echoed in medical literature produced by the U.S. military itself. In a 2007 fact sheet published by the U.S. Army's Chemical Material Agency titled "Characteristics Of Mustard (Blister) Agents," the authors explained the dangers that mustard gas posed to human health if it were to be ignited:

> In a fire, most of the agent would burn up, but some would stay in the smoke. Emergency officials call this smoky cloud and the invisible parts around it a 'plume.' As the plume drifts away from the scene of the accident, small drops of the blister agent may fall to the ground. These liquid drops are called the 'aerosol.' The aerosol is harmful if it makes contact with the skin or if contaminated food or drink is consumed. Some tiny parts of the mustard, called 'vapor,' stay in the plume as it drifts from the accident. Vapor inhalation is harmful. Because the vapor travels farther from the accident than the aerosol, it is the greater danger over a large area. Do not depend on seeing or smelling mustard vapors when asked to take protective action. Invisible mustard vapors will expand beyond any visible smoke, and the faint garlic-like odor of mustard is not a trustworthy sign of a hazard because lower levels of vapor, which are odorless, can be harmful.

While breathing mustard gas aerosol or vapor might not cause immediate and obvious physical damage, the long-term effects can be severe, including internal blistering, blockage of the airways, and chronic respiratory disease.

I knew that from the start of the Iraq War in 2003 to 2009 there was no Defense Department regulation in place requiring the U.S. military or contractors like KBR to do soil or air quality testing. But I wanted to verify that these tests were in fact never conducted at bases in Iraq. I remembered seeing the name of someone who might be able to answer this question for me buried somewhere in the documents I had collected. So I started flipping through my piles of research material and finally found Rick Lamberth's name, a retired Army lieutenant colonel who had served as a combat engineer. Lamberth had also served as a KBR manager in charge of construction in Afghanistan and Iraq, and among his responsibilities was overseeing the rebuilding of some of the former Iraqi military bases bombed in the early days of the war, to make them ready for occupation by U.S. military forces.

When I first got in touch with Lamberth and told him I was investigating the burn pits, he was reluctant to talk to me. He told me he was no longer a KBR employee and he had already testified to the Democratic Policy Committee, an advisory group for Senate Democrats, about the hazards of the burn pits. According to Lamberth, he had subsequently received threats from KBR, telling him to keep his mouth shut to reporters or anyone looking into the burn pits. I could tell when speaking to Lamberth that he was under an enormous amount of pressure. However, I knew he would likely have the answers I needed because of the position he had held with KBR. I told him about the new information I had found, specifically how the burn pits could have been built on ground contaminated by chemical weapons and how thousands of service members' lives depended on finding out the truth. He was quiet for a moment and then said, "Okay, I will answer your questions. What do you want to know?"

I asked Lamberth, "Were there any soil samples taken and tested where the burn pits were constructed? If so, were the tests conducted before or after the burn pits became operational?"

He said, "No, none were taken."

I then asked, "Were there any air quality tests done while the burn pits were operational?"

Again he answered, "No."

"What was burned in the pits?" I asked.

He responded, "Anything and everything. KBR did not care what they burned at Balad, Taji, or any burn pit they operated." He went on to say, "When KBR was constructing Camp Taji, they knew the ground was hot. They knew the ground was probably contaminated. When KBR had to consider the time restraints to get it built and the cost of doing the tests, KBR decided just not to do them."

When Lamberth appeared before the Democratic Policy Committee in November 2009, he testified that he had served in Kuwait, Iraq, and Afghanistan in both military and civilian capacities. While working for KBR, he told the committee, he witnessed KBR employees dump nuclear, biological, and chemical decontamination materials into the pits, as well as biomedical waste, plastics, oil, and tires "in direct violation of military regulations, federal guidelines" and the terms of KBR's contract. He personally witnessed this type of activity occurring in Iraq at such camps as Balad, Taji, Tikrit, Kirkuk, Bucca, and Cropper, and in Afghanistan at Bagram Airfield and Camp Phoenix—all among the largest U.S. bases in these theaters.

When Lamberth tried to report these violations, he testified, "I was told by the head of KBR's health, safety, and environment division to shut up and keep it to myself. At one point, KBR management threatened to sue me for slander if I spoke out about these violations." The huge contractor "was able to get away with this," he added, "because the Army never enforced the applicable standards . . . KBR management would brag that they could get away with doing anything they wanted because the Army could not function without them. KBR figured that even if they did get caught, they had already made more than enough money to pay any fines and still make a profit."

Lamberth believes that he himself is among the victims of the burn pits. He told me that before deploying overseas, he had always been healthy. He joined the military straight out of high school, where he had played three different sports. But since returning home from Iraq in July 2009, he has suffered from a variety of ailments, including skin rashes and shortness of breath. He sometimes spits up bloody mucus. The military will not pay for his medical care, claiming that his conditions are EPTS—"existed prior to service."

Rick Lamberth refused to remain silent. He felt he owed it to his family and to his fellow soldiers to reveal what he knew about the burn pits. As he told the Democratic Policy Committee, "I am testifying here today to let you know that we cannot wait one more day to shut down these burn pits and give proper medical treatment to everyone who has been exposed. We must also stop this from ever happening again."

Chapter 12

Signs and Symptoms

According to CIA and State Department documents, Saddam Hussein's chemical weapons program, Project 922, consisted mostly of mustard and sarin gas production, with mustard gas as the primary WMD that was produced and stockpiled at Iraqi military facilities. To determine if there is a connection between the toxins manufactured by Saddam's chemical war machine and the illnesses of the U.S. service members who were stationed at these former production and storage sites, two very important questions had to be answered. Number one: what was the shelf life for Saddam's chemical weapons? And two: what symptoms would service members exhibit if they were exposed to these toxins?

I checked with both the U.S. Centers for Disease Control and Prevention and the U.S. Army Chemical Materials Agency for answers. I learned that sarin gas is one of the most deadly nerve agents in the world. Created in Germany in 1939, it was mass produced by the Nazi regime, but even Hitler was loath to use it against Allied forces in World War II. Sarin, which attacks a person's central nervous system, is very potent even in very small doses. Those exposed to sarin gas lose control of the muscle function that regulates breathing and usually die within minutes from asphyxia. While sarin is one of the most deadly nerve agents in the world, it degrades very quickly and only has a shelf life of around two months.

Mustard gas, however, is a different story. Created in 1860 by a British scientist, it was not used on a battlefield until World War I, when it was employed by the Germans against British and Canadian forces. Victims of a mustard gas attack generally do not show immediate symptoms. But within twenty-four hours of exposure, the victim will start to have a runny nose as well as intense skin irritation that within hours turns into large, florid blisters. If inhaled, mustard gas is particularly damaging, wreaking havoc on the respiratory system, blistering the lungs and filling them with fluids. Unlike sarin, mustard gas has a very long shelf life; it can stay potent for decades. To this day, for instance, nearly one hundred years after the U.S. military stored and then eventually buried World War I–era canisters of mustard gas at Fort Dix, New Jersey, certain areas of the military installation are still considered contaminated from the buried canisters, and hazardous-material warning signs are still posted in those areas.

Since it seemed that mustard gas, considering its long shelf life, posed the greater danger to U.S. service members in Iraq, I decided to focus on this chemical weapon. I needed to find out more about the long-term effects of mustard gas on those who were exposed to it. And it was necessary to see if those symptoms were consistent with the symptoms of the sick service members who were exposed to burn pits that were built on former chemical weapons facilities.

My research led me to a report published by the Armed Forces Epidemiological Board on July 18, 1996, titled "Long Term Effect Associated with Sub Clinical Exposures to GB and Mustard." The report stated the long-term health effects from mustard gas included a nagging cough, sore throat, wheezing, chest tightness, asthma, bronchitis, influenza, pneumonia, hoarseness, dyspnea, shortness of breath, tumors, and all types of cancers. These symptoms mirrored those of the service members I interviewed who had been stationed at Iraq's former WMD sites. However, I didn't feel the report offered the medical proof needed to say with certainty that the service members were sick due to chemical weapons exposure from the burn pits. The symptoms were not so rare that the only way to get them was through chemical weapons exposure. When I thought about all the garbage that was burned in the burn pits, everything from plastics to medical waste, I thought those items alone could have caused the same symptoms.

I needed solid medical evidence to prove these service members were sick from exposure to chemical contaminants released when the burn pits were built and ignited on poisoned ground, and I was losing faith that I would ever find it. But then came a breakthrough. One night, while I was talking with burn pits health activist Rosie Torres on the phone, she told me about a study on burn pit victims conducted by Dr. Robert Miller, an associate professor of pulmonary and critical care medicine at Vanderbilt University Medical Center in Nashville, Tennessee. Until that point, I had not been able to find any reliable medical studies done on service members regarding burn pit exposure. I phoned Dr. Miller in July 2012, and told him about the research I was doing and about my concerns regarding the health of returning soldiers.

It soon became clear that Dr. Miller shared these concerns. He said that he had subjected the eighty service members in his survey, all of whom came home with burn pit–related health complaints, to intensive scrutiny. The physician evaluated their medical records, looking for any exposure history. He also performed pulmonary-function tests and high-resolution CT scans on all the service members, which are useful in diagnosing lung disease. Out of the eighty men and women in the study, forty-nine also consented to having a lung biopsy performed. Of those forty-nine biopsies, thirty-eight tested positive for a very rare lung disease called constrictive bronchiolitis. While Dr. Miller was very discreet, and would not reveal the names or any identifying information of the service members involved in the study, he did tell me the names of the bases where the service members who underwent the lung biopsies were stationed in Iraq. All thirty-eight service members who tested positive for constrictive bronchiolitis were stationed at one of the six locations that stockpiled or produced chemical weapons.

Shortly after speaking with Dr. Miller, I went to the library and began looking for anything I could find on this extremely uncommon disease. I found out that constrictive bronchiolitis causes the small airways to become compressed and narrowed by lesions and inflammation, making it very difficult to breathe. Though there is no cure for this disease, the patient may qualify for a lung transplant to make them more comfortable.

I found a report on constrictive bronchiolitis published by Dr. Gary Epler, a clinical professor of pulmonary and critical care medicine at Harvard Medical School. According to Dr. Epler's report, there are only five known causes of constrictive bronchiolitis. One cause is exposure to acid-based toxic fumes, such as chlorine, sulfur dioxide, ammonia, and phosgene. In all of the cases where exposure to acid-based toxic fumes was determined to be the cause of the constrictive bronchiolitis, the patients developed the disease while working directly with these chemicals in their raw form in manufacturing plants that were not properly ventilated. The second cause is aspiration of food and other particulates in a very high volume, such as from vomiting. The third cause is ingestion of a leafy vegetable called sauropus androgynus, grown only in Malaysia. The juice of this vegetable was used by local women as a weight control measure. Some of those women developed constrictive bronchiolitis and required lung transplants. A fourth cause is a chemical called diacetyl, which was used in the imitation butter put in microwave popcorn prior to 2002. Similar to exposure of acid-based fumes, the patients who developed constrictive bronchiolitis from this particular chemical worked in a popcorn production facility without proper ventilation.

The fifth and final known cause of constrictive bronchiolitis is exposure to mustard gas.

After reading about the highly unusual ways that people contract constrictive bronchiolitis, it became clear which was the likely culprit in the case of the lung-damaged war veterans. None of them had apparently gone to Malaysia in search of a diet miracle drug, nor had they worked in under-ventilated popcorn factories or other plants where rare toxins were used, and none had aspirated food into their lungs in high volumes. Through a simple process of elimination, I believed I had found the connection. It seemed certain that mustard gas exposure was to blame for the respiratory afflictions suffered by the soldiers in Dr. Miller's study.

It was clear that at least thirty-eight of the soldiers—nearly half of the subjects in the study—were suffering from a rare and incurable disease that they had contracted while serving their country. It took Dr. Robert Miller, a physician who is not affiliated with the Veterans Health Administration or the Department of Defense in any way, to display enough care and compassion to pursue the study and find out why these men and women were suffering. Even after Miller completed his study, the VA and DOD did not follow up and conduct any related medical studies of their own. Instead, DOD interfered with Dr. Miller's work, discouraging service members from participating in his study. Meanwhile, despite the growing body of evidence linking the illnesses suffered by Miller's subjects to the burn pits of Iraq, the VA continues to deny these veterans' disability claims, forcing them to pay for medical treatment out of their own pockets.

Sadly, there is nothing new about this callous pattern of government neglect when it comes to the men and women who risked life and limb for their nation. Each war in the modern era has produced a long list of veterans whose health was scarred by the toxins of war, and who were ignored and rejected when they sought help from Washington.

Chapter 13

Delayed Casualties

The U.S. military has proven time and again that it is reluctant to admit its mistakes. This is especially true when it comes to the possibility of "delayed casualties." During times of war, there are obvious casualties—those who are killed or wounded in action. The DOD is well equipped to handle these all too real and tragic consequences of war. Delayed casualties, on the other hand, result from undetected injuries, problems that manifest themselves over a period of time and are much more difficult to attribute to a specific event. History shows that when it comes to the vast majority of delayed casualties, the Pentagon is at fault—due to negligence, oversight, or a bureaucratic mentality that values budget efficiencies over soldiers' lives. However, over the years, the DOD has consistently denied that these less obvious injuries are a result of war. Sometimes defense officials have even concealed valuable information that would help diagnose, treat, and care for those affected. In certain cases, relevant records and data have been destroyed. The DOD has gone to great lengths to deny the glaring truth when it comes to the hidden injuries of war. Military officials would rather pass the burden of proof onto ailing service members, delaying urgent care and treatment often until it is too late, rather than admit the truth and be held accountable.

This was true during the Vietnam War, when the DOD denied the dangers of exposure to Agent Orange, the herbicide that was used to kill the thick jungle brush around forward operational bases, stripping cover and concealment from attacking North Vietnamese Army and Vietcong soldiers. For years, the DOD continued to claim that the powerful herbicide did not have an impact on veterans' health, even though tens of thousands of returning soldiers reported that they were suffering from a variety of cancers and respiratory disorders. Even as the Agent Orange complaints piled up, the VA continued to deny suffering Vietnam veterans health benefits. In 1985, it was finally confirmed by the EPA that dioxin, one of the major chemicals in Agent Orange, was in fact carcinogenic. (Since then, the National Institute for Occupational Safety and Health and the National Institutes of Health have likewise concluded that dioxin causes cancer.) But even after official findings like this, the VA was reluctant to approve claims for Agent Orange–related disabilities. By 1993, of the over thirty-nine thousand Agent Orange claims that were filed by Vietnam veterans, only four hundred and eighteen were approved.

As with the cancer and birth defect epidemics among the civilian populations of Iraq and Afghanistan, which medical experts connect to the toxic detritus of war, the Vietnamese people also suffered horribly from the U.S. military's widespread use of Agent Orange in their country. According to a 2015 report published by the Aspen Institute titled "What is Agent Orange?", the Red Cross "estimates that three million Vietnamese have been affected by dioxin, including at least 150,000 children born with serious birth defects. Millions of Americans and Vietnamese are still affected, directly and indirectly, by the wartime U.S. spraying of Agent Orange and other herbicides over southern and central Vietnam."

The decision to use Agent Orange on the Vietnamese was so controversial that it led to a debate between the White House, DOD, and State Department. After President John F. Kennedy finally authorized Agent Orange's use in 1961, the U.S. military would ultimately spray about twenty million gallons of chemical herbicides and defoliants like Agent Orange in Vietnam. About 20 percent of all of South Vietnam's forests were sprayed at least once under what was called Operation Ranch Hand.

Beginning in 1966, a series of resolutions were introduced at the UN, alleging that the U.S. military's herbicide program was in violation of the 1925 Geneva Protocol prohibiting chemical and biological warfare. The U.S. government argued that since the defoliation program was intended to wipe out trees to eradicate the enemy's cover, and not to kill people, its widespread herbicide spraying in Vietnam was not in violation of international law.

In a 2002 interview, Robert McNamara himself, secretary of defense under Kennedy and Lyndon Johnson, conceded that the use of Agent Orange and other chemical warfare agents in Vietnam was deeply troubling. McNamara, who publicly wrestled with the morality of the Vietnam War late in his life, stated: "We used Agent Orange—which allegedly killed people. Or we used napalm to burn individuals. Were those in accordance with the accepted rules of war or not? Well, that subject needs a lot more discussion."

In 1977, the UN made it clear that use of toxins like Agent Orange was a war crime when the world body ratified the Environmental Modification Convention, forbidding nations "from engaging in military or any other hostile use of environmental modification techniques having widespread, long-lasting or severe effects as the means of destruction, damage or injury."

Although the DOD is finally starting to take Agent Orange exposure more seriously, officials within the agency itself are saying it may already be too late for many veterans. As then VA Secretary Eric Shinseki put it: "Since my confirmation as secretary [in 2009], I've often asked why, forty years after Agent Orange was last used in Vietnam, we're still trying to determine the health consequences to our veterans who served in the combat theater . . . Veterans who endure a host of health problems deserve timely decisions."

Representative Bob Filner (D-Calif.), then chairman of the House Veterans Affairs Committee, expressed similar concerns in 2009: "Time is running out for these Vietnam veterans. Many are dying from their Agent Orange–related diseases, uncompensated for their sacrifice. If, as a result of service, a veteran was exposed to Agent Orange, and it has resulted in failing health, this country has a moral obligation to care for each veteran the way we promised we would."

Veterans of the Persian Gulf War received the same callous treatment from the DOD when they returned from that war complaining of a new set of mysterious health ailments. In fact, the denial of medical claims related to so-called Gulf War Illness (GWI) paved the way for the burn pit scandal, because many of the health problems that surfaced among veterans of the Gulf War were also related to exposure to chemical weapons.

In 1991, after the Gulf War ended, soldiers began complaining to their DOD doctors and VA representatives about a variety of illnesses that they felt were related to their war service, including fatigue, headaches, joint pain, indigestion, insomnia, dizziness, respiratory disorders, and memory problems. Many of the soldiers believed their illnesses stemmed from the American bombardment and demolition of Iraqi chemical weapons manufacturing facilities and stockpiles. The DOD promptly rejected the soldiers' complaints, stating there was no scientific certainty as to what caused their various problems. Subsequently, the VA sided with the DOD's position and denied disability claims and compensation to sick Gulf War veterans.

Rebuffed by the DOD and VA, Gulf War veterans turned to their representatives in the Senate and Congress, who began investigating their health complaints. The Committee of Government Reform and Oversight, chaired by Congressman Dan Burton (R-Ind.), spearheaded the investigation. Starting in 1996, Burton's committee began hearing testimony from doctors, scientists, and soldiers. A little over a year and a half later, in November 1997, the congressional oversight committee released its report, bluntly titled "Gulf War Veterans' Illnesses: VA, DOD Continue to Resist Strong Evidence Linking Toxic Causes to Chronic Health Effects." The report accused the DOD of gross negligence, stating that defense officials had conveniently lost many of the Gulf War soldiers' medical records, and had lost or destroyed all military records on chemical weapons detection in Iraq during the war. The DOD's bureaucratic stonewalling and sabotage of Gulf War veterans' medical petitions, concluded the committee, "are symptomatic of a system content to presume the Gulf War produced no delayed casualties, and determined to shift the burden of proof onto sick veterans to overcome that presumption."

Finally, in June 21, 1996—under relentless pressure from the committee—the DOD acknowledged that some four hundred soldiers were "presumed exposed" to Iraqi chemical weapons. Under further prodding from the congressional panel, the DOD vastly increased the probable number of exposed soldiers from four hundred to more than ninety-eight thousand. With the DOD's admission of chemical weapon exposure, a door was opened for Gulf War veterans seeking relief from their chronic symptoms and illnesses. But it took years more, and much more medical research and political pressure, before the VA finally started recognizing, treating, and compensating ailing soldiers. Even now, the government's help is often grudging.

The grim story that Gulf War veteran Anthony Hardie told the committee was all too reflective of how returning soldiers from that war were treated, and foretold the experiences of thousands of others who would come home from Afghanistan and Iraq. Here is what Hardie, a seven-year veteran of the Army who now publishes a veterans' health newsletter, told the committee in 2013:

> Gulf War veterans have had unique and special challenges due to the currently medically undiagnosable nature of many of their health conditions. In fact, the data from VA's most recent, December 2007 quarterly Gulf War Veteran Information System (GWVIS) report—which it inexplicably discontinued thereafter—shows that of the 272,215 claims filed by the 696,842 veterans of the 1991 Gulf War (a filing rate of almost forty percent), only 3,149 undiagnosed illness claims, equaling about one percent of all claims filed, have been approved. The fact that only one percent of all Gulf War veterans' claims filed have been approved for 'undiagnosed illness' violates both the letter and the spirit of the Persian Gulf War Veterans

Act of 1998, which was clearly intended to help ill Gulf War veterans receive expedited service-connection for their Gulf-related chronic multi-symptom illness.

Like many Gulf War veterans, I have had chronic sinusitis and a chronic cough since the Gulf. Since my discharge, I have requested again and again for VA to do a lung scope to go into my lungs to see what it looked like, but at every turn was put off, told there were other tests to do first, told there was no reason to do so. Again, my cough has never subsided since it began in February/March 1991.

This spring, after eighteen years, I was finally able to get a bronchoscopy, and its results were yet one more bittersweet revelation—'red, irritated, and angry-looking,' with a diagnosis of one type of chronic obstructive pulmonary disease (COPD), chronic bronchitis. Due to VA's limited scope of Gulf War Illness (GWI) research, I found this bittersweet victory on my own, having gotten the test done privately after having found no support from the VA for getting this test done for my eighteen-year-old chronic cough, despite having firmly and repeatedly requesting it since my very first VA encounter in 1994.

A reasonable person would conclude that all of these conditions, which are anecdotally very common among Gulf War veterans, should be presumptively service-connected and treated by VA under—take your pick—'Gulf War Illness,' exposure to Kuwaiti oil well fire smoke, or exposure to sarin, cyclosarin, or blister-agent vapors. Yet despite all the scientific evidence, VA has not yet made any of these and so many more presumptive conditions for the tens of thousands of ill and ailing Gulf War veterans whose struggles are at least as bad as my own, and due to VA's limited scope of GWI research, there was not and still is not help, or even an understanding of what to look for in us Gulf War veterans.

Like me, many Gulf War veterans battled health issues and struggled to stay in the workforce for years. As I have often said, if it weren't for the military, I wouldn't have been able to keep on struggling, but then again, if it weren't for the military, I wouldn't have had to. Before the military, I was seen as a bright and promising boy, with achievement test scores nearly always in the ninety-ninth percentile, being academically recognized at an early age for reading hundreds of books each year, being selected to represent my high school in quiz bowl, and so on. That factor, combined with my enduring warrior mentality, has meant that my cognitive losses and challenges haven't always been as visible to others who didn't know me before the Gulf War. But for me, it has been extremely painful, with great difficulties in even finishing a book, and short-term and working memory loss that is much worse than most of my elderly relatives and has required major adaptation over many years and reliance on new skills, devices, and assistance.

This pattern of government callousness and neglect, when it comes to treating delayed casualties, has continued throughout the wars in Afghanistan and Iraq. Though the DOD concedes that soldiers were constantly exposed to heavy smoke and ash from the burn pits in those war zones, it continues to deny that this massive exposure was in any way harmful to the men and women serving on those bases. In a July 2008 pamphlet distributed to military personnel and their family members, the Pentagon assured them, "Under most conditions, breathing smoke from burning trash and human waste does not result in any significant risk to short- or long-term health." The pamphlet went on to say that "smoke from burning trash or human waste" was usually made up of relatively harmless "heated gases including carbon monoxide and dioxide, water vapor, and fine particulate matter and hydrocarbons."

The Pentagon's bland reassurances were exposed as grossly wrong the following year, when the U.S. Government Accountability Office (GAO) published its own stunning burn pits report in October 2009. The GAO report provided a great amount of detail about what was burned at the Balad base in Iraq, which consisted of every type of waste: into the Balad pyres went plastics of all kinds, batteries, rubber products, medical waste, and parts of human corpses. The Balad burn pits, which were some of the largest in Iraq, torched roughly one hundred and forty-seven tons of trash a day, seven days a week, for seven straight years, without regulation. Adding to concerns about the Balad pits is the alarming fact that the Balad base sat on the grounds of an old Iraqi military installation that was used by Saddam to produce mustard gas, yet no one ever tested the soil for contamination after the U.S. bombardment of the site.

The negligence on the part of the DOD and military contractor KBR is astounding. The Pentagon's shocking disregard for its troops in Iraq extends to the officer corps as well. As previously noted, among members of the brass who were exposed to the poisonous infernos at Joint Base Balad was none other than Major Beau Biden of the Army National Guard, who served Balad, as well as the equally notorious Camp Victory.

While the military itself has shown little interest in tracking and treating the delayed casualties from the wars in Afghanistan and Iraq, several credible studies have been conducted by physicians independently of the DOD and the VA. One such survey was conducted by Dr. Anthony Szema, chief of the allergy section at the VA Medical Center in Northport, New York, and an assistant professor of medicine and surgery at Stony Brook University on Long Island. His survey, conducted outside of his work with the

VA, revealed that 13 percent of all medical visits by soldiers while they were stationed in Iraq were for new-onset acute respiratory illness. He also found that out of fifteen thousand soldiers he surveyed who were stationed in Iraq, 70 percent complained of respiratory problems.

Another study, conducted by Navy Captain Mark Lyles, who chairs both the medical sciences and biotechnology departments at the Center for Naval Warfare Studies at the Naval War College in Newport, Rhode Island, suggested an even more alarming pattern of burn pit–related sicknesses among returning Afghanistan and Iraq war veterans. Captain Lyles's study, also conducted outside of his work with the DOD, found a 251 percent increase in the rate of neurological disorders among soldiers who were deployed to Iraq, a 47 percent rise in the rate of respiratory ailments, and a 34 percent increase in the rate of cardiovascular disease, all of which Captain Lyles suspects is related to the burn pits.

Both Dr. Szema and Captain Lyles took the results of their work to their respective organizations, yet neither government institution has done anything with the information. The DOD continues to deny there were any health-related issues from the burn pits, and the VA continues to side with the DOD and deny veterans' disability claims.

It's been the same sorry pattern throughout America's military history, long before the war in Vietnam. After World War I, Marine hero Major General Smedley Butler, touring the nation's nightmarish veterans hospitals of the time, condemned them as graveyards of "the living dead." The U.S. government proudly proclaims that it honors the men and women who fight for our nation, but all too often this is simply lip service. In truth, after fighting for their country, these soldiers must return home and fight all over again to receive the care that they deserve.

Chapter 14

The Wheels of Government

It has been said the wheels of government move slowly. But in times of war, Washington can act very quickly. On October 2, 2002, after convincing much of the American public that Saddam Hussein was producing weapons of mass destruction, President George W. Bush asked Congress to give him authorization for the use of military force against Iraq. Just two weeks later, the U.S. House of Representatives and the U.S. Senate approved the president's request. Soon after, the U.S. military deployed over five hundred thousand American service men and women from the active military, the reserves, and the National Guard in preparation for the Iraq invasion. These men and women were uprooted from their normal lives and sent halfway around the world to fight in hostile territory. In total, it took only five months after Bush won congressional authorization for his administration to launch its "Shock and Awe" air assault on March 19, 2003, the prelude to the ground invasion of Iraq.

If the White House and Congress can act so quickly to send hundreds of thousands of men and women to war, why can't they act just as quickly to treat the casualties of war? The foot-dragging bureaucratic obstacles and outright denial of the medical facts that sick veterans inevitably face when they come home from war is a national disgrace. Washington shows again and again that it knows how to make war, but our government consistently refuses to deal with the human wreckage from these wars.

As early as 2008, service members coming home from Afghanistan and Iraq started complaining to their senators and congressional representatives about the illnesses they believed were caused by the overseas burn pits. They also told their representatives that they were being mistreated by DOD and VA doctors and they were being denied medical benefits. But it took four long years for Congress to finally act. On September 12, 2012, a veterans health bill was introduced on the Senate floor, which included a small, first step toward addressing the burn pit medical crisis. The bill called for the creation of a patient registry, so the VA could keep track of veterans who claimed they were ill from the burn pits and could keep the patients informed about significant research and treatment developments regarding burn pit exposure. Three months later, on December 30, 2012, the bill was passed in the Senate, and soon after, President Barack Obama signed the bill into law. The new law stated that the VA had one year to comply and make the registry operational.

It is important to note that throughout the Senate debate over the burn pit registry, DOD and VA officials vocally opposed the proposal. Even after the bill was passed, Curtis McCoy, the undersecretary of Veterans Affairs, expressed doubt that the burn pits really were a health hazard, suggesting that "air pollution, rather than smoke from burn pits, [is] the most concerning potential environmental hazard." VA officials continued to display their contempt for the new law by moving slowly to enforce it. Not until two years after President Obama signed the bill did the VA—under strong pressure from the Senate—finally begin enrolling sick veterans on the burn pit registry.

Though the registry seemed like a step in the right direction, to many ailing veterans, it was too little, too late. It soon became clear that the registry does nothing to help veterans receive medical disability benefits for their related illnesses. In fact, it was modeled on the registries that the VA created to keep track of Agent Orange and Gulf War Illness patients—both of which notoriously failed to alleviate the suffering of those sick veterans.

The Washington bureaucracy is allowed to get away with its shabby treatment of sick veterans, in part because of the incompetence and gullibility of the American press. A long time ago, I came to realize that when it comes to issues concerning war, too many reporters in Washington seem to always take what DOD officials say as the gospel truth, when the fact is, the Pentagon often deceives and misleads the press, routinely covering up awkward facts that would put the military in a bad light.

We saw a glaring example of this when DOD officials and military brass scrambled to cover up the demoralizing truth about the killing of former Arizona Cardinals football star Pat Tillman in Afghanistan on April 22, 2004. Tillman, who patriotically suspended his NFL career to join the U.S. Army after the 9/11 attacks, was accidentally killed in the line of duty by friendly fire. Knowing that the death of such a high-profile soldier at the hands of fellow American troops would be a huge embarrassment for the Pentagon, defense officials lied about the incident and reported that Tillman was killed in an ambush by enemy combatants. The DOD went as far as to award Pat Tillman a Silver Star, writing on the citation that he died "in the line of devastating enemy fire."

I personally witnessed another DOD cover-up while serving with an Army security detail at Guantánamo Bay, when on June 9, 2006, Pentagon officials reported that three Gitmo detainees had committed suicide. I soon discovered that the official story was not true. As I later reported to the Justice Department and to the press, the prisoners were actually killed while undergoing extreme interrogation at a CIA black site on the military compound.

The Washington press corps and members of Congress need to develop a much more skeptical attitude when scandals and crises erupt in the military. They need to look long and hard behind the khaki curtain that is quickly drawn around shameful problems within the armed forces. Instead of taking DOD press releases and internal reports at face value, they need to launch their own investigations and seek out the soldiers and independent medical experts who have bravely risked their careers and livelihoods to shed light on the delayed casualties of war.

When it comes to the burn pits, the top-ranking generals and civilian officials at the Pentagon or CENTCOM have a track record of continually lying or spinning the truth, just as the DOD did throughout the Agent Orange and Gulf War Illness controversies. In my experience as a noncommissioned officer, and after serving twenty years in the military, I can honestly say I would believe the words of a private over a general any day of the week.

Our journalists and politicians need to realize that the real burn pit experts are the men and women on the ground, who have suffered the fallout from these infernos on a daily basis, as well as the few brave doctors who have tried to care for them. These service members, many of whom struggle every day just to breathe, have been scorned and ridiculed by the administrators who should be working to alleviate their suffering. It's up to our public watchdogs in the political arena and the press to make sure they get the treatment they deserve.

Once I had completed my burn pit research, I had to make good on my promise to the ailing veterans who had shared their stories with me. I needed to put my findings in the hands of our political representatives and encourage them to take action. I began close to home.

Chapter 15

Report to the Senate

After thinking it over, I decided that Ron Johnson, the Republican senator from my home state of Wisconsin, would be the right legislator to contact. Johnson, a product of the Tea Party movement, rode that wave into the Senate, defeating Democratic incumbent Russ Feingold in 2010. Johnson had been the CEO of a polyester and plastics manufacturer, which suggested that he might not be sensitive to issues of environmental health and safety; but the Tea Party made a big point of supporting America's troops and a strong national defense. Further, on the Tea Party website, the organization states loudly and clearly that when it comes to federal spending, veterans should be the number-one priority: "First, above all else, our veterans must be taken care of. Let there be not a single penny spent on 'pet projects' until our veterans have access to EVERYTHING they need."

I also believed that Johnson would be eager to show his support for veterans, since the Democrat he turned out of office, Russ Feingold, had a long record of consistently helping service members and veterans during his eighteen years as a Wisconsin senator. In fact, in 2005 Senator Feingold went as far as to delay the deployment of the Wisconsin Army National Guard that was shipping out to Iraq, because the guard units in his state had outdated equipment. Working with Governor Jim Doyle, Feingold made sure that members of the Wisconsin National Guard did not go to war until they were outfitted with the same up-to-date equipment that active duty Army soldiers received. Senator Feingold was also the first senator to raise health questions about the burn pits in Afghanistan and Iraq. I thought Senator Johnson would not want to appear weaker on veterans' issues than his predecessor.

On July 30, 2014, I made the seventy-mile trip from my home in Green Bay to Ron Johnson's state office in Fond du Lac, Wisconsin. Upon arriving at the senator's office, I was escorted into a large room where I met Johnson's point man on military issues, Mark Nielsen. We talked for an hour and a half that day. I explained to him how the VA had not, to this point, acknowledged the burn pits as a major health issue, routinely denying claims from veterans who had been sickened by the toxic smoke and ash. Nielsen said he would personally bring my concerns and my written report to Johnson's attention and I should expect to hear back from the senator's office within two weeks. I left the meeting feeling very optimistic, confident that the burn pit issue was now on Senator Johnson's radar.

Two weeks went by and I heard nothing. I called the senator's office several times and left messages for Mr. Nielsen, but he didn't return any of my calls. After a month went by with no response from Johnson's office, I figured the senator had blown me off, and that he would never take a stand on the burn pit issue. I was wrong—Johnson took a strong stand. It came not in the form of a letter or phone call, but a vote on the Senate floor: nearly eight months after I presented my case to the senator's military affairs aide, Johnson voted to cut President Obama's VA funding proposal by almost one and a half billion dollars.

The cuts Senator Johnson voted for deprived seventy thousand ailing veterans of VA health care. The cuts also curtailed medical research tied to many veterans' projects, including the newly formed burn pit registry. As the *Daily Kos* blog reported, with his vote, Senator Ron Johnson signaled, "It costs too much to fund the VA."

Johnson's vote was not only a direct snub of veterans, but of the Tea Party's stated principles. At the same time he turned a cold shoulder to suffering veterans, Johnson opened the federal checkbook wider for a military boondoggle known as the Ground-based Midcourse Defense system (GMD), which so far has cost taxpayers a whopping $40 billion. The GMD is a missile system that is supposed to protect Americans in the continental United States from foreign missile attacks. The problem with the missile defense system is that it literally does not work. In fact, the defense system has performed so poorly in tests and is so obviously useless that the Pentagon doesn't want it. One recently retired senior military official, who served under both Presidents Bush and Obama, said: "The system is not reliable. We took a system that was still in development, it was a prototype, and it was declared to be operational for political reasons."

Why would a penny-pinching Tea Party stalwart like Senator Johnson support a hugely expensive missile system that does not work, and at the same time cut VA funding for treatment and benefits that veterans so desperately need? The answer may be veterans, for the most part, don't wield a lot of financial clout in the political arena, whereas Raytheon, the primary defense contractor on the GMD fiasco, is a large financial contributor to the Tea Party and to Senator Johnson's 2010 campaign and his 2016 reelection race.

I had made a promise to my fellow veterans, vowing to make the burn pit health crisis a national issue. But as I examined Johnson's voting record on veterans' issues—as well as the votes of other Tea Party members in Congress—I felt that we'd been played. Despite its flag-waving rhetoric, the Tea Party clearly didn't give a damn about the men and women who served our country. As I pored over congressional voting records, the facts were plain to see. It was Republican members of the House and Senate—including the Tea Party zealots—who consistently voted for VA cuts, while Democrats supported veterans' spending.

While Congress, on both sides of the aisle, has been all too ineffectual when it comes to helping sick veterans, there have been a few standouts on Capitol Hill who have tried to help victims of the burn pits. Among these congressional warriors are current and former members of the House of Representatives such as: Tim Bishop, Maurice Hinchey, and John Hall of New York; Raúl Grijalva of Arizona; Dennis Kucinich of Ohio; Jim McGovern of Massachusetts; Chellie Pingree of Maine; Carol Shea-Porter of New Hampshire; Steve Cohen of Tennessee; and Shelley Berkley of Nevada. On the Senate side, Russ Feingold, Evan Bayh and Ron Wyden also performed heroically. These members of Congress—all of whom are Democrats—began writing letters to the DOD as early as 2008, demanding answers about why so many veterans were coming home sick. Unfortunately, there are just too few men and women like this in the House and Senate—politicians who not only like to have their pictures taken with our troops, but actually do something for them when they are in need. It is important to note that of all thirteen senators and congressional representatives I mentioned above, only five of them are still in office.

Chapter 16

"Embrace the Suck"

In February 2004, while I was in the Army National Guard, my unit was sent on a one-month military operation to the island of Hokkaido, the largest and northernmost island of Japan, located twenty-six miles east of Siberia. Our mission was to train members of the Japanese Defense Force, many of whom were being deployed to Iraq in MOUT (military operations on urban terrain) warfare tactics and combat patrols. The weather on Hokkaido can be Siberian in its brutality, especially during the winter months, and my stay there was no exception. Temperatures plunged below zero during most of our tour of duty and the island was bombarded with four feet of snow. We slept in heated canvas tents, but the heaters were unreliable and only worked half the time. I would often wake up in my sleeping bag in the middle of the night feeling like I was freezing to death. During the day, we worked long hours and conducted most of our training outside. Our uniforms would become wet from snow and sweat. Whenever we stopped moving, even for a short period of time, our damp uniforms would start to freeze, making us even colder.

One day during training, I was standing alone, shivering, likely looking as miserable as I felt. One of the other soldiers I deployed with walked over to me and said, "Hickman, embrace the suck." I laughed and we started joking about how cold and miserable we were. It didn't take long for the joking to turn into shenanigans. We started diving in the snow, making snow angels, and throwing snowballs at one another. The entire time we were playing around, the Japanese soldiers were watching us with bewildered looks on their faces.

"Embrace the suck." This is a phrase commonly used by American soldiers to inspire motivation in one another when dealing with the horrible conditions that soldiers sometimes face during military operations. The strange humor shared by U.S. service members is something that makes them unique. Whenever I've been attached to foreign military forces, I always notice that our twisted sense of humor, the way American soldiers laugh at misery, is something troops from other nations just don't understand.

This odd humor has been with our military for a long time. In Vietnam, soldiers would watch as U.S. planes swooped overhead, spraying clouds of poisonous Agent Orange over the lush tropical greenery on the battleground. They watched as the chemicals killed everything around them and knew deep down those chemicals could not possibly be good for them. But they laughed and joked about it anyway, telling each other that when they were back in the States starting families, they would have three-headed babies. These men were laughing in the face of death. Embrace the suck.

During the wars in Afghanistan and Iraq, the poison was not dropped from planes. It wafted in smoky clouds from the nearby burn pits—over 200 of them in Iraq alone—enveloping the barracks, offices, and food stations where thousands of American soldiers went about their daily business. But even while the service members were breathing in the noxious fumes round-the-clock, they found a way to make light of it. At Camp Taji, when a new morale, welfare, and recreation facility was built near one of the worst pits, the rec hall was jokingly named by the soldiers, "The Burn Pit." Like the soldiers who came before them in Vietnam, these soldiers were laughing in the face of death. And now death has come for many of them.

The delayed casualties from Afghanistan and Iraq continue to pile up:

* Staff Sergeant Danielle Nienajadlo, U.S. Army, died on March 20, 2009, at age thirty-one after being diagnosed with acute myelogenous leukemia, leaving behind three children, ages three, eight, and ten, and a husband who is also in the military. After passing her pre-deployment physical with flying colors, Nienajadlo began complaining of the foul air where she was stationed, at the notorious Balad base in Iraq. "She'd go back to the hooch at night to go to bed and cough up these black chunks," recalled her mother, Lindsay Weidman.

* Sergeant Amanda Downing, U.S. Army, died on January 22, 2011, after succumbing to adrenal cancer at age twenty-four.

* Sergeant Brandon Matic, U.S. Marines, died on May 24, 2013, of esophageal cancer at age twenty-six.

* Technical Sergeant Jessica Sweet, U.S. Air Force, died February 12, 2009, after losing her battle with acute myelogenous leukemia at age thirty.

* Specialist Andrew Rounds, U.S. Army, died October 17, 2007, from acute myelogenous leukemia at the age of twenty-two.

* Staff Sergeant Steven Ochs, U.S. Army, died July 12, 2008, from acute myelogenous leukemia at age thirty-two.

* Staff Sergeant David Thomas, U.S. Army, died in late June 2014 from lung cancer at age forty-six.

* Specialist Dominick Liguori, U.S. Army, died May 11, 2012, from a rare lung disease at the age of thirty-one.

* Colonel David McCracken, U.S. Army, died September 2, 2011, from brain cancer at the age of forty-six.

The list goes on and on. Like so many others, the above service members were in good health before being deployed to Afghanistan and Iraq. After returning home sick, they all came to believe that their illnesses were a legacy of the burn pits overseas. And all of them were denied VA help for their suffering.

Tens of thousands of other veterans continue to struggle with their burn pit–related health problems, with little or no aid from the government that sent them into harm's way. Their chronic, debilitating illnesses are heaping financial and emotional stress on these veterans and their families. Many of them are going broke trying to pay their medical bills and losing their homes to foreclosure. Families are falling apart. Young veterans are dying in hospital beds, leaving huge medical debts for their grieving husbands, wives, and children.

These veterans of the wars in Afghanistan and Iraq should not be forced to wait decades for help like Vietnam vets were. They need help now. Doctors, scientists, environmental engineers, sick veterans them-selves—they have all made a convincing case that tens of thousands of American soldiers were poisoned through the negligence of the military and KBR, the huge con-tractor that is responsible for so much of the military's daily operations. Washington has heard the pleas of its suffering soldiers. But so far the government response to these sick men and women amounts to nothing more than, "Embrace the suck."

Symptoms and diseases of case study subjects

acute myelogenous
  leukemia
allergies
anxiety
apnea
asthma
auto immune system
  conditions
back cancer
back pain
basil cell carcinoma
bleeding gums
bleeding stomach lining
blisters
blood clots
blurred vision
brain tumor

brain tumors
breast cancer
breathing difficulties
breathing problems
bronchitis
burning in the back of
  throat
carcinoma
cardiac issues
chest infection
chest pain
chest tightness
chronic kidney disease
chronic myeloid leukemia
chronic pain syndrome
chronic respiratory illness
cold sweats

cold-like symptoms
colds
colon cancer
compromised respiratory
    function
congestion
COPD
cramps
cysts on right lung
decrease in bladder function
decrease in bowel function
decreased lung capacity
degenerative tissue disease
depression
dermographism urticaria
diabetes
diarrhea
difficulty breathing
digestive issues
dry cough
emphysema
enlarged spleen
epididymitis
essential thrombocythemia
eye issues
facial droop
facial scars
fatigue
fever
fibromyalgia
GI distress
GI issues
giant bullae

glaucoma
hardened bronchial tubes in
    lungs
hardened nodules in lungs
headache syndrome
headaches
heart attack
high blood pressure
Hodgkins lymphoma
horizontal nystagmus
IBS
infertility
inflammation in eyes
insomnia
intestinal issues
irritated throat
joint pain
kidney blockage
kidney function problems
labored breathing
laryngitis
lesions
ligament issues
loss of taste
low blood O2 levels
lower back pain
lung calcification
lung cancer
lymph nodes
lymphoma
memory loss
memory problems
metallic taste in mouth

migraines
multiple sclerosis
muscle ache
muscle issues
muscle spasms
myocardial diffusion
nasal polyps
nausea
neck pain
neurological damage
neurological disorder
neuropathy
non-Hodgkins lymphoma
numbing and swelling of
   hands and feet
numbness
open sores
pain during breathing
Parkinson's Disease
pericarditis
photophobia
pigmented keratosis
pleural fibrosis
pneumonia
polycythemia vera
prostate cancer
PTSD
pulmonary complications
rash
rashes
reactive airway disease
reduced ability to speak
reduced lung capacity

respiratory infections
respiratory issues
restrictive airway disease
restrictive lung disease
rheumatoid arthritis
scarring in left lung
seminoma cancer
serious skin rash
sexual dysfunction
shoulder pain
shortness of breath
sinus infection
sinus pressure
sinusitis
skin bumps
skin cancer
skin damage
skin rashes
sleep apnea
sleep disorder
sleep disturbances
sleeping issues
slurred speech
smaller bullae
sore joints
sores
Stage 2 Hodgkins
   lymphoma
stage 3 ovarian cancer
stomach issues
stomach pain
swelling

thickening of the bladder
　walls
throat infection
throat irritation
tingling in arms
tingling in hands and feet
tumors
epithelioid
　hemangioendothelioma
upper respiratory infections

upper respiratory
　problems
uterine cancer
vertical nystagmus
vision deficit
vision problems
vomiting
weight loss
white spots
white spotted rash

For more information

News reports

"Veterans Administration Ignores Delayed Casualties of War Caused by Open Air Burn Pits in Iraq and Afghanistan," Report by Global Research Solutions, January 2016

"Leaked Memo: Afghan 'Burn Pit' Could Wreck Troops' Hearts, Lungs" by Spencer Ackerman, *Wired* magazine, May 22, 2012: http://www.wired.com/2012/05/bagram-health-risk/

"The Secret Casualties of Iraq's Abandoned Chemical Weapons" by C.J. Chivers, *New York Times*, October 14, 2014: http://www.nytimes.com/interactive/2014/10/14/world/middleeast/us-casualties-of-iraq-chemical-weapons.html?_r=0

"A fatal wait: Veterans languish and die on a VA hospital's secret list," by Scott Bronstein and Drew Griffin, CNN Exclusive, April 23, 2104: http://www.cnn.com/2014/04/23/health/veterans-dying-health-care-delays/

"Iraq: War's legacy of cancer" by Dahr Jamail, *Al-Jazeera*, March 15, 2013: http://www.aljazeera.com/ indepth/features/2013/03/2013315171951838638.html

"Iraqi Birth Defects Covered Up?" by Jeena Shah, *The Huffington Post*, October 4, 2013: http://www.huffingtonpost.com/ the-center-for-constitutional-rights/iraqi-birth-defects-cover_b_4046442.html

"Cancer rates on the rise in Afghanistan, kills over 16,000 people annually," *1tvnews*, February 4, 2015: www. afghanistan/en titled http://www.1tvnews.af/en/ news/afghanistan/15126-cancer-rates-on-the-rise-in-afghanistan-kills-over-16000-people-annually

"The Iraq War's Real Legacy" by the Organization of Woman's Freedom in Iraq, August 26, 2011: http://www. owfi.info/EN/article/the-iraq-wars-real-legacy/

Government reports, testimony

U.S. Government Accountability Office report, "Afghanistan and Iraq: DOD Should Improve Adherence to Its Guidance on Open Pit Burning and Solid Waste Management," October 2010 http://www.gao.gov/new.items/d1163.pdf

Dr. Anthony Szema's testimony on the dangers of burn pits to the Senate Democratic Policy Committee, November 6, 2009: http://www.dpc.senate.gov/hearings/hearing50/ szema.pdf

Medical studies

"Constrictive Bronchiolitis in Soldiers Returning from Iraq and Afghanistan," by Dr. Robert F. Miller et al, *The New England Journal of Medicine*, July 21, 2011: http://www. nejm.org/doi/full/10.1056/NEJMoa1101388?viewType= Print&&&

"Constrictive Bronchiolitis Obliterans: What Do We Know About This Fibrotic Airway Disease?" by Dr. Gary R. Epler, *The Journal of the American College Of Chest Physicians,* February 2, 2008: http://69.36.35.38/accp/pccsu/constrictive-bronchiolitis-obliterans-what-do-we-know-about-fibrotic-airway-disease?page=0,3

Academic studies, lectures

Statistical study on burn pit victims who were stationed in Iraq: a report by Seton Hall University School of Law's Center for Policy and Research, January 2016

"Environmental Poisoning of Iraq: Why Academics Must Speak Out," lecture by Dr. Mozhgan Savabieasfahani at the University of Washington, October 24, 2014 https://www.youtube.com/watch?v=2B0Hlw7uE7g

Organizations:

Burn Pits 360
4450 Beachcraft Road
Robstown, Texas 78380
Phone: 361-816-4015
http://www.burnpits360.org/

The Sergeant Thomas Joseph Sullivan Center
1250 Connecticut Avenue NW, Suite 200
Washington, DC 20036
Phone: 1-855-748-7855
http://sgtsullivancenter.org/

Burn Pits Action Center
https://sites.google.com/site/burnpits/

Acknowledgments

I would like to thank all of the military service members and veterans that I have interviewed or who have come forward in the media to speak about the burn pits. Without their courage, this book would not have been possible. I would also like to give special thanks to Professor Mark Denbeaux and Seton Hall University School of Law's Center for Policy and Research, for their study and hard work on all the issues concerning the burn pits. I would also like to thank my favorite writer, Dick Russell, for encouraging me to write the book.

The following people were invaluable to the completion of this book and I thank them deeply for their friendship and support: C. Williams, Doris and Richard Anderson, Ross B., Jules H., Sara R., Ashley Y., Alicia D., Kelly H., Jason P., and Heather F. Last but not least, I would like to thank David Talbot and Tony Lyons and all the incredible people at Hot Books/Skyhorse Publishing. It has truly been an honor working with you all.